Buon Appetito Toronto!

Buon Appetito Toronto!

Mansfield Press
Italian Chamber of Commerce of Ontario
Toronto/Milan/2014

Copyright © Italian Chamber
of Commerce of Ontario 2013
All rights reserved Printed in Canada

Book Team

Publisher and concept: Corrado Paina, ICCO
Editor: Deborah Verginella
Project Coordinator: Marta Scipolo
Photography: Rick O'Brien
Graphic Design: Denis De Klerck
Interviews: Marta Scipolo and Deborah Verginella*
    [* Barone, McEwan, Milne-Allan, Barato]
Transcriptions: Amanda Coletta
Proofreaders: Denis De Klerck, Ally Fleming
Website: Phiroze Dennis
Cover Photos: Rick O'Brien, Bruno Crescia
Additional photographs: Bruno Crescia, Chuckman Toronto Nostalgia, Denis De Klerck, Piera Pugliese, Marta Scipolo, Scotiabank Archives, Shutterstock, Emilia Valentini, Deborah Verginella

Advisory Committee:

Corrado Paina, George Visintin, Rosanna Caira, Ron Sedran, Claudio Gemmiti, Walter Simone.

Thanks to the Board of Directors of the Italian Chamber of Commerce of Ontario

Tony Altomare, Bruno Amadi, Alberta Cefis, Enrico De Pasquale, Pat Pelliccione, Marisa Piattelli, Domenic Primucci, Joe Ragusa, Ron Sedran, George Visintin.

Thanks to the staff of the Italian Chamber of Commerce of Ontario

Claudia Barbiero, Chiara Bombardieri, Tony Cipriani, Elena Dell'Osbel, Corrado Paina, Gabriella Silano, Giovanni Silvestri, Tiziana Tedesco, Giorgio Tinelli.

Thanks to the generous businesses, organizations and individuals that helped sponsor the creation of Buon Appetito Toronto!

Bennett Jones LLP, Forest Contractors Ltd., Greater Toronto Marketing Alliance, Italpasta Limited, Jan K. Overweel Ltd., Regione Lazio-Sviluppo Lazio, Magnotta Winery, Marchio Ospitalità Italiana, Marisa Piattelli, Monte Carlo Inns, Pizza Nova, Saputo Dairy Products Canada, Scotiabank, Sobeys, Unico Inc. - Primo Foods.

Library and Archives Canada Cataloguing in Publication

Buon appetito Toronto! / edited by the Italian
Chamber of Commerce of Ontario.

ISBN 978-1-77126-032-9 (pbk.)

1. Cooking, Italian. 2. Food—Italy. 3. Italian Canadians—
Ontario--Toronto--Food. I. Italian Chamber of Commerce
of Ontario, editor of compilation

TX723.B86 2013   641.5945   C2013-906564-4

Mansfield Press Inc.
25 Mansfield Avenue,
Toronto, Ontario, Canada M6J 2A9
Publisher: Denis De Klerck
www.mansfieldpress.net

Table of Contents

TUTTI A TAVOLA! *Rosanna Caira* / 7
MOTHER ELEGY *Luciano Iacobelli* / 13
PAPA'S TRIPE *Gianna Patriarca* /13
THE ITALIAN WINE EXPERIENCE *Tony Aspler* / 15
ER PIATTO PREFERITO DE PAPÀ
Bruna Di Giuseppe-Bertoni / 19
MUSKOKA PASTA *Domenico Capilongo* / 19
BAR ITALIA *Eugene Barone* / 21
   BAR MERCURIO / 25
BERTOZZI IMPORTING *Elvira Bertozzi* / 27
   B ESPRESSO BAR / 33
BIAGIO RISTORANTE *Biagio Vinci* / 35
   CAFÉ DIPLOMATICO / 41
BUCA OSTERIA & ENOTECA *Robert Gentile* / 43
   CALIFORNIA SANDWICHES / 51
CAMPAGNOLO *Craig Harding* / 53
COPPI *Alessandro Scotto* / 61
FAEMA *Mike Di Donato* / 69
   CAMARRA / 73
TRATTORIA GIANCARLO
Eugenia Barato & Jason Barato / 75
   COMMISSO BAKERY / 81
GRANO *Roberto Martella* / 83
ITALPASTA LIMITED *Joseph Vitale* / 91
   CONTINENTAL NOODLES / 97
LA FENICE *Rocco Fosco* / 99
.GELATO SIMPLY ITALIAN / 105
LETTIERI AND HERO CERTIFIED BURGERS *John Lettieri* / 107

GIO RANA'S REALLY REALLY NICE RESTAURANT / 113
LIBERTY ENTERTAINMENT GROUP *Nick Di Donato* / 115
LONGO'S *Anthony Longo* / 123
MAGNOTTA WINERY *Rossana Magnotta* / 129
   IL GATTO NERO / 135
FABBRICA *Mark McEwan* / 137
   INNISKILLIN WINES / 143
MISTURA *Massimo Capra* / 145
   LA PALOMA / 151
NOCE *Guido Saldini* / 153
PAGANELLI'S RISOTTERIA *Gabriele Paganelli* / 161
JAN K. OVERWEEL AND EMMA FOOD IMPORTERS
Pat and Arthur Pelliccione Sr. / 169
   MERCATTO / 175
PIZZERIA LIBRETTO AND ENOTECA SOCIALE
Max Rimaldi and Rocco Agostino / 177
NOTA BENE *Franco Prevedello* / 185
PIZZA NOVA *Domenic & Sam Primucci* / 193
   SICILIAN ICE CREAM / 199
PUSATERI'S *John Mastroianni* / 201
   VESUVIO / 207
SOTTO SOTTO *Marisa Rocca* / 209
   VIA ALLEGRO / 215
TERRONI *Cosimo Mammoliti* / 217
UNICO AND PRIMO FOODS *John Porco* / 225
   ZAZA / 231
ZUCCA *Andrew Milne-Allan* / 233

Vesuvio Circa 1963

TUTTI A TAVOLA!

By Rosanna Caira

In 1974, Joanne Kates's first restaurant review appeared in The Globe and Mail and only then because she had convinced the feature's editor that there was a need for a food critic and a weekly restaurant review in this city. That inaugural review, of George Minden's revolutionary restaurant Noodles on Bloor Street West, marked a new era in Toronto's dining scene. Kates wrote,

"Thanks to Noodles, Toronto's Italian food is no longer limited to lasagna and pizza with side trips to veal marsala and fettuccine a la carbonara. At Noodles there's shrimp and green pea soup, fresh Dover sole in a delicate anchovy, capers and tarragon butter.... Pasta is made from scratch every day and then cooked to order ... You won't find a fresher noodle in Canada today. Or tomorrow, probably." (Globe and Mail, April 22, 1974.)

In the 1950s, the period of the biggest wave of Italian immigration, the city affectionately known as "Hogtown" was a culinary landscape of roast beef, potatoes and canned peas and soft white bread. The city's few restaurants closed nightly by 10 p.m. and if you had a craving to dine out on Sunday—well, most of the restaurants were closed, and the few that were open had to contend with archaic liquor laws.

As Italians settled into their newly adopted country they shared homes with like-minded paesani, found jobs, and earnestly began their new lives. Food remained central: moving beyond sustenance and transcending social joy, it symbolized success. In Italy many of these immigrants struggled to put food on their tables. But here, where jobs were plentiful, they could suddenly buy much of what their hearts, and stomachs, desired.

"We should not forget," John Dickie states in *Delizia*, "that most of the people who emigrated did so precisely because they were excluded from Italy's civilization of the table. Polenta and other dishes of the poor were miserable daily reminders of that exclusion. Food certainly shaped the identity of peasant emigrants from Italy, but envy, anger and ambition—not nostalgia—marked their attitudes to eating when they departed, and those feelings turned food into a badge of who they were once they arrived." So, while many immigrants had rarely eaten meat in Italy because they could not afford to, once in Canada, eating meat meant they had finally arrived.

Italians quickly turned to the neighbourhood grocery store run by fellow Italians for foodstuffs that reminded them of home, and in doing so introduced the city to a vast array of new products. Pasquale Bros. on King St. W., the precursor to today's ubiquitous specialty store, opened in 1917. Owned by Edward Pasquale and his son-in-law, Henry Madott, the family-run business was one among the first to provide Italians with their preferred cheese, olives and antipasti. And in the heart of Little Italy, at College and Ossington, grocery stores such as Johnny Lombardi's and White Rose, owned by brothers Joe and Rocco Bertucci, were examples of places where Italians could find staples such as pasta made by Lancia-Bravo, Unico canned tomatoes or dried legumi that would produce cheap and plentiful meals like the pasta e fagioli they had at home. As they migrated north to St. Clair, establishments like Ferlisi emerged selling prosciutto, salumi, giardiniera and olives, and a bounty of fruit and produce that Italians missed and could scarcely get elsewhere.

Italians wasted little time before transplanting their tried-and-true traditions to the new land. As they saved enough money for their first homes, the resourceful new Canadians found a solution to the lack of flavourful produce they eagerly sought: manicured lawns were replaced with abundant vegetable gardens (orti) that included the beloved tomato, zucchini, eggplant, and peppers, vegetables the average Torontonian of the time had never heard of. Later, as Italians returned to Italy they would smuggle radicchio, arugula and Swiss chard seeds, multiplying the variety of their harvest. Their Canadian neighbours must have looked on in wonder at the wooden stakes supporting tomato plants, and that wonder into perplexity as zucchini vines climbed and flowered into strange golden blossoms collected, battered, fried into crisp morsels, and (gasp!), eaten! And how to describe their reaction at dandelions picked from city lawns and parks that would be tossed into salads? Or the homemade sausages and sopressata, pancetta and prosciutto curing in their basement cantine? The self-consciousness they may have felt could not dislodge the memory of the food they loved. They may have been new Canadians but their culinary allegiance was unshakably Italian.

And so, a distinctly Italian restaurant culture emerged and Italian food quickly became an intrinsic part of city dining. One of Toronto's early pioneers was Vesuvio's, the first pizzeria and spaghetti house. Rocco Pugliese and his sons, Domenic and Ettore, opened Vesuvio in 1957 on Dundas St. West and almost overnight it set the standard for tasty pizza in the city's west end. The family arrived via

New York and, not surprisingly, popularized the New York-style 'pie' they had learned to make from a New York bakery called Vesuvio's. The two brothers influenced half of Toronto's restaurant industry in some way with their introduction to the secrets of pizza making.

Others quickly followed. Camarra opened in 1958 on Dufferin Street, south of Lawrence, in what was quickly becoming a suburban Italian enclave. The restaurant, started by Elisa Camarra Valentini, her brother Livio (who went on to open Maestro), and their mother Domenica, highlighted pizza, pasta and panini. On College Street, the city's original Little Italy, Il Gatto Nero and Regina's Pizzeria became beloved fixtures. And San Francisco Foods and California Sandwiches gave birth to the transcultural cult of the Italian veal sandwich, a breaded cutlet with tomato sauce spilling out of a crusty bun, inspiring urban myths of fedexed sandwiches to New York City. Further north on St. Clair, crusty Italian bread emerged from the ovens of Tre Mari, and dolci and gelato were produced at La Paloma. Long before Starbucks created coffee culture for the masses, Italian men sat in cafes. Here they sipped espresso and watched soccer matches as women prepared the noonday meal.

Power Grocery Store 1958. Photograph courtesy of the Scotiabank Archives

As the men made their way home, they bought fresh bread and *paste* (pastries) for dessert.

"There were quite a lot of Italian restaurants back then," recalls Charles Grieco, who, along with his father, John, opened La Scala restaurant in 1962, the first fine-dining Italian restaurant in Toronto. "But most of them were mom-and-pop shops that featured red meat sauces and Chianti wine. We stepped away from that to create a destination and brought to the city Italian accents not before seen," stressing the restaurant made a conscious decision to not offer spaghetti and meatballs. Instead it highlighted handmade, never-before-seen lasagna, ravioli, cannelloni, as well as the classic veal and beef dishes of Italy. Toronto food critic James Chatto applauded, "It was a bold move to do posh that wasn't French." La Scala introduced diners to wines from Antinori, Folonari and Ruffino and was the first to bring the wines of Gaja to Toronto. "The city was ready for something different, something elegant and that focus happened to be Italian," recalls Grieco, who today heads up the Ontario Hostelry Institute.

Not until the mid '70s did the new wave of Italian restaurants begin to surface, dramatically altering the image of Italian cuisine across the continent. In New York, pasta dishes were suddenly getting attention in French restaurants, olive oil made its debut as an ingredient in dishes, slowly replacing the butter and cream typically associated with French cuisine, and restaurateurs like Sirio Maccioni from Le Cirque "were helping people realize the potential of Italian food," says David Kamp in *The United States of Arugula*, "introducing New York to dishes like pasta primavera and products like radicchio from Treviso, even displaying the red bunches of leaves, still in their shipping crates, in the dining room." Within months, American cookbook author Ed Giobbi recalls, "every three- and four-star restaurant in New York had radicchio on the menu."

Here, Noodles ushered in that era. George Minden, owner of the posh Windsor Arms Hotel, wanted to showcase chef Herbert Sonzogni's knowledge of Italian food. The restaurant décor, as much as the menu, marked a dramatic change in the idea of Italian restaurants. Joanne Kates noted the milestone: "Noodles was Toronto's first Italian restaurant that broke the mould of checked tablecloths, spaghetti and candles in Chianti bottles." All chrome and pink neon and leather, Noodles was sleek and clean and the food represented a modern approach to Italian food—whether it was the ethereal gnocchi al gorgonzola, pasta in walnut pesto, or cooked-to-order risotto. When the charming Dante Rota took over in 1985, the restaurant was setting new standards in dining. Rota had immigrated to Canada via England and worked with Sonzogni at the Windsor Arms.

David Adjey, now a celebrity chef, apprenticed under Rota, and recalls how instrumental his mentor was in changing the perception of Italian food. Rota focused "on dishes that were hundreds of years old. If it was a traditional dish of Rome, he cooked it that way," says Adjey. "He didn't modify it. He didn't bastardize it. He made the dish as it was supposed to be. He taught me that food, ingredients and dishes have integrity, and you, as a chef, have to respect that. It's not up to you to put your flair in it." Noodles became a hotbed for developing new talent, including Terroni's Cosimo Mammoliti, who got his start there as a food runner.

By the early '80s, Toronto, now the country's biggest city and financial centre, was in the throes of a culinary revolution. Franco Prevedello, who had worked under Charles Grieco at La Scala, opened a trio of restaurants that would change how many, in a city edging towards cosmopolitanism, viewed Italian food. "[Franco] reinvented Toronto fine dining with his high-energy restaurants Biffi, Pronto and Centro," says Kates.

Prevedello started his career in Toronto in the 1970s as a waiter, grounding himself in the fundamentals of great service in the city's most storied restaurants, including the Westbury Hotel and Quo Vadis. He knew that for a restaurant to be truly successful, the owner had to be there to oversee all aspects of great hospitality. Prevedello left an indelible mark on the culinary fabric, opening Pronto in 1981, Centro in 1987 and Splendido in 1991. Pronto was unlike anything the city had seen. "We had to do something very different to be noticed," recalls Prevedello. Located on Mount Pleasant Avenue, away from the bustling downtown core but convenient for the affluent Rosedale clientele, it was hip, loud, and bustling, and featured menu items most Canadians were unfamiliar with: fresh-made pasta in variations that included fettucine Natasha, with salmon and caviar and spaghetti with Pernod.

"If the modern Italian restaurant was invented in Milan in the 1970s," says Chatto, "it was Franco who brought it to Toronto, though his influences were certainly filtered through San Francisco and New York. People loved the mood, the razzle-dazzle and having Franco there to look after them."

By the time Prevedello opened Centro at Yonge and Lawrence, Italian food incorporated many of the trends taking place south of the border. "I wanted to do an Italian restaurant with a touch of California, and slowly develop into Italian regional cuisine, develop flavour and taste that's regional," he told Foodservice and Hospitality in 1988. "I like to call it Italian with a sprinkle of California parsley," he quipped. "What fueled the popularity of Italian was its approachability and freshness of ingredients," says Prevedello. It became popular, he says, because "it took away the snobbery of dining."

"Prevedello picked up where Noodles left off and taught us modern Italian sophistication: Pasta without tomato sauce! Fresh fish! Risotto," recalls Kates. And, he introduced oenophiles to the Super Tuscan wines. Even the most basic of Italian staples like pizza appeared on the menu in inventive ways. Prevedello offered thin appetizer-style pizzas made in wood-burning ovens imported from Italy and popularized by Wolfgang Puck in California. He imported a new breed of Italian chef to help him spread the gospel, chefs like Massimo Collavini who went on to helm Cibo, an immensely popular Rosedale eatery, and Raffaelo Ferraro who started at Pronto and then migrated to Centro. Michael Bonacini (who now heads the Oliver Bonacini restaurant empire), Marc Thuet and David Lee are just some of the notable chefs who helmed the kitchen at Centro. And while Thuet and Lee are not Italian, they honour Italy's culinary traditions.

By the time the '90s arrived, Italian cuisine had knocked French fare from its 'ne plus ultra' post. This fuelled the fever for restaurants like Prego della Piazza where the food was stellar but so was its glamour and exclusivity (a bottle of mineral water cost 12 dollars!). Owned by transplanted Boston native Michael Carlevale, who opened the upscale Bersani & Carlevale sandwich chain in the late 70s, Prego was the place to see—it was the unofficial headquarters of celebrities attending The Festival of Festivals (now TIFF)—and be seen. Prego also introduced us to mustachioed Massimo Capra, owner of Mistura and several other restaurants, and now one of the celebrity chefs on the Food Network.

Today, there's a new casual approach to Italian food that also reflects the full integration of the Italian community in Toronto. Thanks to a new breed of restaurateur like Rocco Agostino and Max Rimaldi, the team behind Pizzeria Libretto and Enoteca Sociale, Italian staples like pizza are finding new fans. Line-ups at Pizzeria Libretto and Queen Margherita (to name just two) are standard as Torontonians debate the merits of Roman (crispy and thin) and Neapolitan pizza (softer and blistered). Pizza chains too are seeking a slice of authenticity. Last year, Pizza Nova, celebrating its 50th year, introduced Focaccia Barese, a flatbread that carries an authentic designation conferred by the region of Puglia.

Today's Italian chefs are re-creating their grandmother's recipes and serving dishes up with a twist. "It's almost as though they are consciously stepping back into the immigrant experience," postulates Chatto. In fact, in 2009, chef Rob Gentile of Buca, who cut his culinary teeth under top toque

Mark McEwan at North 44, was heralded for his unique salumi bar, set in the middle of the restaurant and featuring a range of products from house-cured sausage to lardo. And this return to the past can be seen in the geographical choices of these new establishments. While many of the restaurants of the '80s and '90s surfaced in the city's toniest areas, recent openings are in the old neighbourhoods: Ossington and Dundas Street, and College Street are once again prime destinations for Italian food now that rustic Italian rules supreme.

More than fifty years after Italians arrived on the biggest wave of immigration this country has ever seen, Italian food has been embraced by all and is available in all parts of the city and beyond. Increased travel, food magazines, blogs, and specialty TV channels like The Food Network have entrenched the vocabulary of Italian food. "I don't think there's a restaurant in this city that has not been influenced by Italian," boasts Grieco. And, "Italian food is no longer being produced just in Italian restaurants; it's an integrated reality."

Italian food products, from the vast number of olive oils from various regions of Italy, to a wide range of Italian breads, to the myriad sausages classified by region, from the Barese to the Calabrese and everything in between, line the aisles of Pusateri's, Bruno's, the Cheese Boutique, and McEwan's. Chains such as Longo's and Fortino's have become havens for all things Italian. Talk to any Torontonian and their product knowledge of all things Italian is now vast and impressive. Mark McEwan, an admitted Italophile, once told a room full of culinary students at George Brown College, "I want to be Italian in my next life." Could the postwar immigrants who cultivated their orti ever have imagined it?

Rosanna Caira is the editor and publisher of Foodservice and Hospitality, *a national magazine serving the $65-billion restaurant industry in Canada. She was one of the many thousand Italians who made the long and arduous trek from Italy to Canada on the Vulcania during the large wave of Italian immigration in 1960.*

Photograph courtesy of Chuckman Toronto Nostalgia

MOTHER ELEGY

Mother rolled her own dough
and made her own pasta.
The sauce, made from backyard tomatoes,
simmered daily on the elements.
Little red splotches covered the stove top.
She couldn't understand
why I rejected the home cooking:
tired of the food I'd known all my life,
I ate sandwiches in restaurants.
But one Sunday afternoon, I stayed home
and stared at her as she shelled peas,
stared at the light reflecting
off the metal bowl, stared around the kitchen,
the arrangement of utensils, and I thought
   to myself,
my God, what a picture this is:
When my mother wasn't looking,
I dipped my finger in the sauce
and an old appetite returned.
That same day she complained of an ache.
A few weeks later we were told the worst.
A few months more, she was
an emaciated memory.
After the funeral, I sat on the back porch
and my grief was a bright red geranium,
the weeds were the garden's condolence,
the morning glories clung desperately
to the railing, and I was hungry for the meals
I had once refused to eat.

Luciano Iacobelli

PAPA'S TRIPE

Tonino Meats is still there
on Rogers by Silverthorn
papa and me went every Friday
after he cashed the paycheck
bought chicken and steak
mortadella for Mary
and always his favourite
tripe
papa loved tripe
mama hated the smell
when it boiled away
getting whiter and whiter
she'd never cook it
it was papa's delight
he'd slice it in long thin strips
the onions and garlic and celery
the jars of tomato and basil
the olive oil
i was the *sous* chef at his side
stirring and tasting
it would simmer for hours
on the stove

in the dish he would drown it in
parmigiano
"alla romana" he'd say
and sit with the wine and the spoon
my ginger ale
and the smile
i learned to love it with him

after he died
no one made tripe anymore
i remember the recipe
have tried it at times
but without papa
it never seems to taste the same

Gianna Patriarca

THE ITALIAN WINE EXPERIENCE

By Tony Aspler

There is an old joke that dates back to the 1969 lunar landing that the first thing Neil Armstrong saw after his "one small step for a man" was a Neapolitan making pizza.

So pervasive is Italian food culture in North America that it helped to create the taste for fine Italian wine outside its own community. Angelo Gaja, the great Barbaresco producer, once told me the reason why Italian wines sold so well in Canada and the US was because of the proliferation of Italian restaurants throughout the continent. No other wine growing nation is blessed with the loyal support of emigrant restaurateurs and the generations that followed them. Figures from the last census in 2006 suggest that 4.6 per cent of the Canadian population consider themselves to be of Italian origin; and if they don't actually own a restaurant they frequent the dining establishments of those who do.

According to Roberto Martella, the proprietor of Grano, "It was the Italian immigrants who carried the flag with them internationally and Italian products and foodstuffs and, of course, wine followed. They established a toehold in the rest of the world through the Italian communities." Even if a restaurant is not ethnic Italian, if it has pasta on the menu it has to carry Italian wines.

I would like to propose a theory that the success of Italian wines in the Ontario market is due—in large measure—to one man, one wine and one book in the watershed year of 1980.

But first, a little history. Toronto has always been the magnet for Italian immigrants but the Italian wine experience in the 1950s was far different from what it is now. Consider wine buying in Ontario in the '50s. The Temperance movement was a powerful force in those days and the LCBO, in deference to the prevailing sentiment, issued cards to consumers who wanted to purchase beverage alcohol. There was a maximum number of bottles one consumer was allowed to buy per month. The same restrictions applied to wine importing agents. Saverio (Sam) Schiralli, who opened his Toronto-based importing business in 1952, had to borrow the cards of friends and relatives so he could buy enough samples to give to restaurants in order to promote his wines. By the 1960s Schiralli was offering Barolo Fontanafredda, Chianti Bertolli in the straw flask bottle, Negrar Valpolicella and Lambrusco Castelvetro Chiarli.

By the mid-1970s the Schiralli agency had the two best-selling Italian wines on the market—Colli Albani and Castelli Romani in screw top litre bottles or 2000mL—that were destined to become the house wine of virtually every Italian restaurant in the city. These basic table wines, along with Rosso and Bianco Fiore, Gambellara and Verdicchio, would monopolize Toronto's wine lists well into the 1980s.

In those years, anecdotal evidence suggests that there was as much wine being produced in the basements of Italian homes as was sold by the LCBO. Italian immigrants made wine with California grapes that were picked unripe and matured as they were trucked-in to Toronto. But according to Donald Ziraldo, the co-founder of Inniskillin, "the younger generation of Italians didn't want to make wine in their basement or garage. They weren't up to dealing with fruit flies." (Ziraldo, incidentally, might well take the credit for the extraordinary popularity of Pinot Grigio today. He brought in the first Pinot Grigio vines from Friuli in the late 1980s and planted them in his Niagara vineyard.)

Roberto Martella remembers his late father-in-law making wine from those trucked-in California grapes. "It was an important introduction to many young people, the children and grandchildren of Italian immigrants who now are professionals and wine-buying people who certainly don't make wine that way any longer. It was important for them to understand that wine is food. When we first opened [Grano] we used to serve wine in glass tumblers. We wanted to make a statement that this is how Italians viewed wine at the table and culturally. 'Wine as food' is something Italians bring to the mix."

Wine shopping in the 1970s continued to be a dreary undertaking throughout the province. If you walked into an LCBO outlet in those days you could easily have thought you had wandered into the waiting room of a local railway station as not a single bottle was visible. And while the indignity of ration cards were done away with in 1962, the wine buying experience was not much better in the '70s. You had to scan the boards of drab LCBO stores to see what wines were available. Once you had made a selection you filled in a piece of paper with the name of the wine and the product number, handed it across the counter and paid for it. The employee disappeared and returned with a brown paper bag. He—invariably it was a he—slipped the bottle out of the bag by its neck to give you a surreptitious glance at the label. And then he slid it back. To our current sensibilities the entire transaction was more like purchasing porn.

Toronto's Italian restaurants in the 1950s, '60s and '70s were mainly Mom and Pop establishments serving a menu of spaghetti and meatballs, lasagna, cannelloni, and the occasional osso buco. On the table would be a straw-covered Chianti fiasco supporting a stalactite of melted multi-coloured candle wax. The Chianti bottle became the symbol for Italian wine. The fiasco, as it was called in Italian, competed with the Mateus Rosé bottle as Toronto restaurateurs' candelabra of choice. In 1959 the LCBO listed seven Italian wines (two in half bottles): five of these were Chiantis, the other two, an Orvieto and a Marsala. By 1963 the Italian category had increased to thirteen: Barolo, Valpolicella, Verdicchio, and Lacryma Christi were added to the Chiantis.

The first Italian restaurant that offered a fine dining experience in Toronto was opened in 1962 by John Grieco and his son, Charles. La Scala would become a favourite haunt of Queen's Park politicians and Bay Street financiers. "The food was upscale Northern Italian cuisine," recalls Charles Grieco. "We didn't have spaghetti and meat balls. We did all of the specialty veal dishes that very few people in Toronto had experienced before. We grilled things rather than just fried them. At the same time people began to discover that Italy had more than Chianti and Valpolicella. We began to see the Super Tuscans, we began to see better wines from Piedmont and Friuli. At that point in time Sicily was not in the picture; it came later."

When cook book author, journalist, and teacher Bonnie Stern was training as a chef in 1971 she recalls that French food still reigned supreme in Toronto. Lucy Waverman, another of Toronto's eminent teaching cooks, equates the improvement in Italian food with a demand for better wines. "As people got more interested in wine—and because we have a wealthy Italian population here—they wanted their wines brought in for them too. Franco Prevedello was one of the first to bring in good Italian wines."

And that brings me to the man, the wine and the book that created a sea change in Toronto's Italian food and wine scene in 1980. In 1965 Franco Prevedello, an immigrant from the hill town of Asolo in Veneto, was working as a waiter at the Westbury Hotel. The wine list here was basically French. He then became the maître d' at John Arena's Winston's for five years, the most popular haute cuisine restaurant in Toronto that catered largely to a celebrity clientele. (Winston's had been named after Winston Churchill in 1946 to appeal to WASP sensibilities.) Here too, the wine list was also almost exclusively French. While still at Winston's Franco opened Quo Vadis, and after four years as catering director of the Trillium restaurant at Ontario Place, he opened the first of his break-out restaurants—Biffi on Mount Pleasant Road.

One of the wines on Biffi's list was supplied by a Bahamian importer, the late Colin Carruthers, the first agent to take a serious interest in fine Italian wines. In 1979 Carruthers imported Masi Campofiorin 1974, a blend of Corvina, Rondinella, and Molinara. Campofiorin was the first Valpolicella to be made by the now ubiquitous Ripasso method which allows the wine to re-ferment on the residual skins of Amarone to give it more extract and richness. This wine, the first that Roberto Martella put on his list when he opened Grano in 1986, is one of the few quality Italian wines that is still continuously available at the LCBO after nearly 35 years.

1980 saw the publication of a book called *Vino—The Wines and Winemakers of Italy* by an American journalist named Burton Anderson who worked for the Rome Daily American from 1962 to 1967 and now lives in Italy. This seminal work unlocked the mysteries of Italian wines and pointed the curious oenophile to the country's best producers. And it was also in 1980 that Franco Prevedello and his fellow restaurateurs visited Verona to attend the annual Vinitaly wine fair. Their mission was to source new and exciting wines for their establishments. In the course of these trips Franco introduced his clientele to producers such as Anselmi, Quintarelli, Maculan, Primo Franco, Biondi Santi, Avignonesi, Felsina, Conterno, and Gaja. The following year he opened Pronto across the road from Biffi. And then, in 1987, came his most ambitious and most successful venture, Centro on Yonge Street. There would be other Prevedello restaurants (Terra, Acrobat, Splendido, Acqua, Acrobat bis, Nota Bene) and those that he consulted to, but the hallmark of each venture was the range and quality of its wine list. And along with the increased quality of the wines came impeccable wine service with Riedel stemware and decanters to match. (Riedel was the first glassmaker to design the shape of the glass according to the character of the wine.)

The 1980s were exciting years to be in the restaurant business in Toronto, especially for Italians. Apart from Franco's establishments you could enjoy great Italian cuisine and matching wines at Vittorio Trattoria, Cibo, Noodles, Celestino and Frank Faigo's cuisine at the Windsor Arms Hotel. "It was called Northern Italian cuisine then," says Franco. "Just to keep a little difference [from the spaghetti restaurants]. The influence of the beautiful Italian food was very southern, peasant-like. Nowadays, chefs are going back to the generic Italian food but at a higher level. There is no Northern and Southern Italian food. Italian food is regional and every region has its specialty. We called it Northern Italian just to differentiate ourselves from so-called generic Italian restaurants."

This plethora of fine dining establishments, according to food and wine writer James Chatto (whose book *The Man Who Ate Toronto* chronicles those years) was the start of the new, fresh approach to Italian cuisine. "What I love about the Italian restaurant scene is that there are so many ways of doing it," Chatto will tell you. "You had Kit Kat, so casual, and Grano with its intelligent way of looking at food and integrating it into Italian culture. Then you had Bersani and Carlevale which turned into Prego. Massimo Capra was the chef. In the 1990s there was this good, solid middle ground with restaurants like Noce and Il Molino, Il Posto, Zucca, Mistura, Coppi and Paese, all with good wine lists at a time when the whole idea of French restaurants was dwindling almost to nothing. Phil Sabatino at Via Allegro, and Opus, both with monster wine lists. Guy Rubino at Luce. Terroni, Five Doors North, Tavola Calda. Young sophisticated chefs who are cooking their grandmother's recipes, almost taking it back to that post-immigrant feel. Buca, Aria—these are restaurateurs who were determined to build a great Italian wine list."

While the Italian bistros and trattorias of the 1990s relied on the fashionable regions of Tuscany, Piedmont, and Veneto from which to source their wines, a new breed of trained sommeliers began to look further afield to Puglia, Sicily, Trentino Alto Adige, Oltrepó Pavese, and Lombardy. Things were loosening up. "I remember in the mid-1990s Franco staged a dinner on a Sunday evening at Centro with Angelo Gaja," recalls Roberto Martella, "and I was asked to say a few words. I reminded the guests that it wasn't that many years ago when one could not have found a restaurant open on a Sunday evening in Toronto and find this kind of quality of fare and this kind of service. The whole notion of a formal restaurant didn't exist as such before."

The influence of Italy is all-persuasive in Toronto's dining experience today. Charles Grieco summed it up best when he told me, "You can't go into a restaurant without seeing some technique, some style, some flavour that comes from Italian cuisine. The impact is so huge, whether we're talking about Californian-Italian or Italian, the influences cut across the board. I don't think there is anyone's menu that doesn't have influences that can be described as being Italian. And that also goes for the wines too."

Today, Italian wine in Ontario is a quarter of a billion dollar business. Such is the popularity of wines from Italy that in the fiscal year 2012/13, there were 2,127,488, 9-litre cases of Italian wine (red, white, rosé, and sparkling) imported into the province. Sixteen years ago the LCBO carried 731 skus. This past year the figure was 1,724. Ontario's love affair with Italian wine just gets more passionate and much has to do with the awakening Anglo-Saxon understanding that wine is as important to the table as bread and salt.

Tony Aspler has been writing about wine for over thirty years. He was the wine columnist for the Toronto Star *for twenty-one years and has authored sixteen books on wine and food, including* The Wine Atlas of Canada, Vintage Canada, The Wine Lover's Companion, The Wine Lover Cooks *and* Travels With My Corkscrew. *Tony's latest book is,* Canadian Wineries.

In December 2007, Tony was awarded the Order of Canada.

Photo: Shutterstock

ER PIATTO PREFERITO DE PAPÀ

Mi padre nun vedeva l'ora
Der Venerdì.
Ogni settima come te manna
er patreterno er Venerdì,
mi madre faceva er piatto
preferito de papà.
Solo dall'odore l'occhi je se
l'uminavono e je veniva
n' sorriso allegro e poi diceva:
"Se magna?"
Nun c'era pasto se nun faceva l'acqua
frizzante co la bustina de idrolitina.
Nun ce potete crede, sola a Roma fanno 'sta
pasta da anni fa in qua. "Quant'è bona!"
Er destino fu che se ne semo annati
da Roma e dalla patria nostra. Emigrati semo.
Ma venne anche qua er giorno della pacchia
quanno mi madre je fece 'na sorpresa, nun era
un Venerdì, era Domenica.
Je fece trovà er piatto preferito
così nun sentiva 'a nostalgia de Roma
e de l'Italia.
Io che je so fija pe me è l'stesso.
Più sce penso e più me viè 'na voja
e da quanno lui nun c'e sta più,
nun faccio caso se è Domenica or' Venerdì.
Prendo 'na bottiglia d'acqua frizzante pe'a sete
e poi me gusto 'na= spaghettata de cascio e pepe!

Preparazione in parole mie.

Cucina i spaghetti dentro 'na cazzarola, ner mentre grattuggia er pecorino e mettelo dentro 'na scotella, aggiungi anche er pepe. Mettece dentro un bicchiere de acqua de cottura e gira er cacio e pepe fino a che nun se fa 'na crema. Quanno i spaghetti so ardenti, scolali e lascia sempre un po' de acqua de cottura. Pija i spaghetti e metteli dentro a scotella cor cacio e pepe, e gira bene bene fino a che nun so cremosi.

Se so asciutti metteci un po' de acqua de cottura...
gira sempre bene fino a che nun so belli cremosi.
Serveli subito calli calli che so più boni.

E questo era er piatto preferito de papà.

Bruna Di Giuseppe-Bertoni

MUSKOKA PASTA

the backseat a rotini of laughter
as we cut through the parmigiano snow
carving deeper into the winter afternoon
the tortellini moon creeping in the rearview

the power's out in the hotel
we stumble through the cannelloni hallway
like overcooked linguine

the four of us cuddle in the ravioli bed
in lasagna layers of pajamas
telling stories of minestrone superheroes
until the gnocchi light bulbs pop back on

Domenico Capilongo

BAR ITALIA
an interview with Eugene Barone

What is your first memory of food?

I remember I was four or five. I was walking in the cold rain with my mother to deliver a hot meal to her recently widowed friend outside of our town in Calabria. It was a pot of "Lagane e Ceci," homemade tagliatelle with a sauce of slow-cooked chickpeas, a touch of tomato and pork skin. The ceci were cooked in a clay pot over the fire and I remember they held the fire's smoky flavour. I still crave that dish.

What were your beginnings in the food business?

When I was seven years old in Sartano, Italy, my sister and husband had a bar/cafe and I helped out. To this day, at fifty-six years old, I cannot taste lemon gelato without thinking of my time in that place.

At eight I started selling pop in Trinity Bellwoods park, at sixteen years old I was a barista at the Dip [Cafe Diplomatico on College Street]. And when I was twenty-three I opened Milk Nuts & Things on College (the only variety store ever to be written up by Joanne Kates in the Globe and Mail!). When I was thirty years old I bought Bar Italia. I always found a way to relate to people through serving food in one way or another. It has always made me happy.

How would you describe your vision for Bar Italia?

My idea was to combine everything that I loved about Italian culture, all the things that I knew and remembered, filtered through coffee, liquors, food, and boccette. I wanted to create and share an atmosphere that was based on what I felt as a young Italian-Canadian. I wanted Bar Italia to be an inclusive place for men and women, for Italians and for everyone else.

Are there memories of Bar Italia that stand out in your mind?

There are too many to mention! That's another book! A favourite memory of College St. would have to be, in 1984, sitting on milk crates outside Milk Nuts & Things with my good friend Pasquale Lanzillotto. We had to call a taxi service for a friend to get a cab and it took forever to get there. I said to him, "One day, there will be cabs lined up on this street, like in Yorkville." Ten years later, there were.

As for Bar Italia, before I bought it, I was a regular, playing pool, and had my daily espresso there. When it came up for sale, I couldn't let it go.

I also remember then Governor General, Adrienne Clarkson, giving me grief about not serving Canadian bottled water….

What do you see as the future of Italian food in the city?

Toronto diners have had the pleasure of many great Italian and Italophile restaurateurs and chefs who have contributed to an exceptional food scene over the past twenty years. I, for one, have done my best to share my own personal regional Italian favourites, and we have all learned from each other. The Toronto diner I am familiar with will not settle for the American-Italian version of the cuisine. The future of Italian food in this city will always be in the search for the best raw ingredients that Italy and Canada can produce. The food has to be authentic and honest.

Which ingredient or dishes were turning points for the culinary scene here?

Arugula. Most Canadians didn't know what it was back in the early '90s, now it's commonplace on menus and in grocery stores. Having olive oil with bread instead of butter was exotic at the time.

And thanks to Andrew Milne-Allan, panini and crostini on the dinner menu. It was unheard of—and an instant success for Bar Italia.

If you closed your eyes and imagined you were in Italy, what would you be eating right now?

I would be in front of a plate of freshly sliced mortadella, spicy provolone with olives, and crusty bread.

Why do you think Italian cuisine holds such mass appeal?

Simplicity, seasonal ingredients, the versatility of pasta. Bright, bold flavours that do not need to be messed with. It's consistent. As food trends come and go, customers always find their way back to the reliable comfort of Italian food.

You have just closed a chapter with your second successful restaurant, Rosina. If you were to open a restaurant today, what would the concept be?

Today I would open a place with a chalkboard menu, offering two or three dishes that change daily, and with the seasons, the way a trattoria commonly would in Italy. House-made antipasti, pasta, and lots of fresh seafood. Low inventory, little overhead. And, of course, a wine list featuring Italy and Ontario.

Did your business influence the products suppliers sourced?

Of course. Good suppliers pay attention to what you are having success with. I know they often felt pride when their products did well for us, and used Bar Italia as a selling point for their other clients.

Do you still go to Italy for inspiration?

I went every year until my parents passed away. It is different for me now. I hope to take my family one day soon. Going to Italy has always been a key source of inspiration for me, I always return with such appreciation for the culture. And that type of inspiration was largely responsible for the success of Bar Italia.

Eugene Barone (pictured with Andrew Milne-Allan) was the owner of Bar Italia from 1987 to 2005. Joe Bonavota is the current owner.

BAR MERCURIO & L'ESPRESSO BAR MERCURIO

270 Bloor St. W. and 321 Bloor St. W.

Owner: Joe Mercurio

Opened: 1997

Highlights: wood oven pizza, gnocchi alla rucola

Fact: Bar Mercurio inhabits what was once a diner, the historic haunt of U of T students and physicians in the Medical Arts Building at Bloor and St. George. L'Espresso Bar Mercurio re-creates the experience of an Italian bar for the large academic, intellectual and professional community that comprises the neighbourhood.

Photo: Marta Scipolo

BERTOZZI IMPORTING

an interview with Elvira Bertozzi

Tell me about the history of Bertozzi.

EB: It was my husband's business. He came from Italy, from Parma, and had a dream to import Parmigiano Reggiano. In 1956 he incorporated the company in Montreal.

His father, Tommaso, produced Parmigiano Reggiano in the early 20th century. They also made prosciutto di Parma. They fed the by-products of the Parmigiano Reggiano to the pigs and then made prosciutto di Parma. At that time, the consortium of prosciutto di Parma was almost non-existent. It was the cheese producers who also produced prosciutto. After the war, it was very difficult for a young person to have any opportunities so my husband and some of his friends talked about immigrating to Canada. He came. Two of his friends stayed behind in Italy. He had some money which he earned in Venezuela on his way to Canada. He was working during the night and selling Parmigiano Reggiano during the day. Men who came to Canada from Italy at that time found it very hard because they didn't have anyone. They were a breed of young men who were determined, strong, and had a vision and a dream.

When he began the business what was available in the marketplace?

EB: We are talking about 1956. You had the first wave of postwar Italian immigration. There were many single men. They didn't know English and were working menial jobs. My husband had gone to university in Bologna so he was an educated man but there were many who were not and they just decided to open stores near where they lived. That's how Little Italy was created. My husband was selling cheese to those little shops. First in Montreal because that's where we were living, but then we moved to Toronto. To go back to your question, first he imported Parmigiano Reggiano and then he began to import other cheeses that the market and the Italian consumer demanded. Those cheeses were pecorino romano, then crotonese, and then canestrato. I didn't know anything about food at the time. I was interested in classical literature and had attended a liceo classico in Montreal, so my education was quite different. I remember we used to go to Italian restaurants often in Montreal. When we first met we would always go to this Italian restaurant

in Montreal owned by Lisa Magnani who ended up being a witness at our wedding. They made the most authentic gnocchi, lasagna, and semifreddo that I have ever encountered, even in Italy. It was the most authentic Italian food you could find in Montreal at the time. We didn't go as much once the children arrived. Anyway, my husband was importing basic Italian cheeses at the time as well as grana padano, but then he wanted to expand. We couldn't import the fresh cheeses because the airfare was so expensive and it was difficult to ensure freshness when it was coming by air. So we began to import jams from the Alto-Adige region, extra-virgin olive oil from Lucca and vegetables in oil and vinegar. There was no aceto balsamico at the time or pesto or sundried tomatoes. At that time, only the basic Italian foods were known and were imported. They were the ones that the immigrants wanted. Beyond that, it was very limited.

Immigrants weren't interested in the other products?

EB: No. Keep in mind that Italy is divided regionally. Most of the immigrants that came were from southern Italy and then those that did come from the north were from Friuli and Veneto. We brought those things that they were familiar with and wanted. But my husband was very adventurous and wanted to explore. At Christmastime we started to import panettone. At the time, we had panettone Alemagna and torrone for Christmas as well. Then the Italian government made panettone public so we could bring in more types. But now, of course, panettone is available all the time and not just at Christmastime, which has ruined the market for it a bit. It's too bad. For us, the main thing was to bring the top quality products here and to Toronto. Slowly, the market evolved.

Was the Toronto market different than the Montreal market in terms of the demand for Italian food products?

EB: It was more or less the same at that time. I went to do the Italian grocery shopping so I remember. I used to go to this store on St. Clair and Rogers. It wasn't such a nice place, but it was close enough that I could walk there with my kids. That was the area where Italians congregated. It wasn't that different from Montreal. Even the restaurant scene was similar. My husband used to take me to restaurants only for my birthday because we weren't able to find a restaurant like the one my friend Magnani had in Montreal. My husband was a very traditional man. He wanted me to be at home, take care of the children, and prepare the meals. Men worked so hard at the time. Home was like a refuge. When my husband came home we would all be waiting for him at the dinner table. We would congregate as a family and talk together; it was an important moment. Unfortunately, now it has changed. Women work hard now. Even back then, some women had the dual role of doing the traditional things and then working as well. It wasn't easy, but I was fortunate because my husband allowed me to stay home. He would bring me the best things to cook. His mother was an excellent cook. When we went to Parma, his hometown, in the summer, I learned how to cook many of the things from that region. My signature dish is tortelli di erbette. I just love it. And you used to eat them for the vigilia di Natale because you couldn't eat meat. I learned to do it very well. It was a tradition. I think every woman brought some tradition from Italy to the family.

As the company grew were you still selective about the products you imported?

EB: Yes, but a lot of it was based on what the Italian consumer wanted and bringing the best we could for the Italians here. When my husband died we continued to bring the best Italian food to the

Canadian market. At first, yes, our focus was on the Italian consumer only, but slowly, it evolved. When we opened in Montreal, Italian immigrants were not travelling back to Italy very often and neither were many Canadians. That has all changed now. Travelling has really helped a lot. If you stop along the highway sometimes in Italy, you can come across some good food. It's not the same as what you might find in the big cities, but it is still better than the food you find along the highway rest stops here. I remember one day driving from Torino to Parma we stopped along the highway and the food was very good. Tourists experience good Italian food and when they come back they want these products. We started to bring them those products.

When did you join the business?

EB: When my husband died. Before he died I was indirectly involved. He was a heavy smoker. I didn't smoke so he would always let me taste the products: I was the palate. Before the company really grew I would also send the orders to Italy. Do you know how we sent them? By telegram. We didn't have computers or anything like that and the mail could take forever, so we would send a telegram. It was the only way to officially transmit an order.

What do you appreciate most about Italian food? What makes it appealing?

EB: For me it is how easy it is to prepare. The geography and history of Italy allows every region of Italy to have a different cuisine. Variety is the beauty of Italian cuisine. You have to use the best ingredients to make the best dish. The raw material has to be the best that it can be. That's why we wanted to bring the best products to Canada. The freshness, the variety, and the simplicity are what is important. If you have basic knowledge of Italian food preparation, you can evolve. It's like poetry: you need to know terza rima to know Dante and then to know Quasimodo. In cuisine, you need to know traditional Italian cuisine and the basics and then you can evolve.

When did you know your business was going to grow and be a success?

EB: We were growing and we knew this was our path. We didn't know whether we were going to be big or not. We didn't care about that. We created our niche. Competition is healthy in a way but it can also be destructive for a company. We knew where to concentrate, we knew what our customers wanted, and we wanted to maintain our integrity. With our olive oil, the one we imported was more expensive than the others. It was for a reason though: it was better! With the emergence of the Mediterranean diet there was an explosion of olive oil. We were very careful to bring in olive oil that was made in Italy. We made sure that the olives were grown on Italian soil and not somewhere else and then packaged in Italy. It was very important.

How do you stay competitive without compromising your standards? Do you choose to be selective with not only your products but who you supply?

EB: Yes. We don't deal very much with restaurants because they tend to want only cheap things. We focus more on grocery stores and little specialty shops across Canada. We send salesmen all over Canada. We've expanded, but selectively. My husband wanted to give an advantage to the smaller shops because he realized they were our bread and butter. He always preferred to deal with the smaller shops as opposed to the very large supermarkets.

Looking at the restaurant scene in Toronto, do you think people have a true understanding of authentic Italian food?

EB: It's a bit difficult to say. You do still need to educate people. Olive oil is a good example. Olive oil is the juice of the olive. You need to have a good, healthy olive to produce good olive oil and this starts with the olive grove. Drainage, insect control, and cleanliness are very important. The olive absorbs everything so it's a very tricky process. When the consumer goes to the market, there are hundreds of brands of olive oil. Sometimes they don't understand the differences between them or which ones are best: they have to be educated about it. If you have the passion, you must

continuously educate in this business. Our education starts with the customer and with the salespeople.

Bertozzi is a family company. Have you transmitted these values and principles to the next generation?

EB: Absolutely. My husband had ethical values. We try very hard to maintain them. Integrity is very important—integrity when dealing with the suppliers, the customers, and the consumers. This is how you create a name for yourself and build trust. It is very important.

I'm curious to know what your favourite dish is: is it the same as your signature dish?

EB: Yes. Actually, you know what? We started importing frozen foods from Emilia Romagna. I couldn't find a good stuffed egg pasta on the Italian market. I found one, but it was frozen. It was very good. It's Michelin star restaurant material. I am so excited about this product. When I came to Canada there was a lot of frozen food: there were frozen dinners, but that was never really something you could bring to the table. It originated in the States but it developed in Italy. I will use an analogy: the car was developed in the States under Ford, but it was in Italy that the Ferrari was produced. It's the same thing with food. Frozen food originated in North America, but Italian frozen food is incredible. They've adapted tradition to modern life.

So you are importing these frozen products?

EB: Yes, we started in April. It will take generations I think before they can really become huge. I have different dreams. When I was young, my husband and the people who came after the war worked so hard so women couldn't have a career many times. I couldn't have a career. Now things are different.

Do you have any regrets about following this path?

EB: I followed my children's education. When they finished high school I decided I wanted to go back to university. I entered an English literature program. I loved it because I loved the challenge and because I loved literature and history. Those were the best years of my life. I looked forward to lectures all the time. It's never too late to have a good education. You need to have a good knowledge of the Bible and Scripture and then you build on top of that with mythology and things like that. It's the same with food culture.

B ESPRESSO BAR

111 Queen St. E., Suite 102,
273 Bloor St. W., Royal Conservatory of Music Atrium

Owned: Bruno Colozza

Opened: 2004

Highlight: espresso blends are created exclusively for b espresso bar (espresso roast, Italian roast, dark roast, decaffeinated roast)

Quote: *"Espresso should be to the coffee bean what Prada, Hermès and Valentino are to fashion..."*

Photo: Deborah Verginella

BIAGIO RISTORANTE

an interview with Biagio Vinci

When did you open Biagio?

BV: I started when I was seventeen and my idea was to become a good restaurateur. When I left Calabria in 1955 it was the first time I put my feet on a train. This train took me all the way to a small town in Switzerland, Estavayer-le-Lac. There, my passion for the restaurant business began. I was trained by a small family. The restaurant was run by the mother, the father, and his sisters. I was the fourth son. They adopted me for eight months. I was the bus boy but I did a little bit of everything. From there I moved to the beautiful city of Lausanne on Lac Léman. There, I worked at a grocery store and learned about the products you need to make a good dish. Next, I worked at the Grand Hôtel in Lausanne for about a year and a half, doing jobs in both the kitchen and the dining room. I wanted to know things about all departments. After that I went to a small town in the Alps and did two seasons in the dining room. Again, with the hard and tough Swiss management, you learn a lot about how to run a restaurant.

Were these Italian restaurants?

BV: No, they were typical Swiss restaurants. Then I became confused, I didn't know what to do. I was twenty-three. I wanted more education about restaurants and searched for a good school. The second-best school in Europe at the time was in Stresa. I could not afford the price they were asking monthly, so I worked for another year in Switzerland and saved enough money to be able to go the next year. I took a nine-month course on Hotel and Restaurant Management. When I graduated I went back to Switzerland for six months, and then to a small restaurant in Paris where I stayed for three months. I decided to learn at least another two languages to allow me to move around; I was fluent in French, so I moved to London. I worked in a beautiful hotel where I stayed for almost two and a half years. I was trying to put into practice everything that I had learned in school. In London, I met my wife.

Is she Italian?

BV: No, she's British. I didn't want to take her to Italy and I didn't want to stay in London. London was great to work in, but we decided to choose another country. We went to South Africa. It didn't work. We tried Australia, but it was too far. Finally, we decided to come to Canada. If we didn't like it we knew that we could always go back to Europe. We are still here after fifty years! Toronto was tough in the beginning, this was the mid-1960s. It was tough to find a job. It was still a meat and potatoes city. We decided to stay a couple of months to try to make money to go back but then opportunity knocked. I had the good fortune to meet a friend of mine, Dr. Carbone, who was part of a daily takeout service. He offered me a partnership in the place. It was one of the best daily takeout places in Canada and it served French food. I took the opportunity and started to work and manage this place. I had a catering service which grew quickly and I started to add Italian dishes which slowly became more accepted by the public.

Which dishes did you introduce?

BV: Cannelloni, lasagna, veal—typical Italian dishes. Then we added carpaccio and things started to go really, really well. My dream was to have a great and unique restaurant in Toronto where I could develop my skills. One day while walking down King Street, I spotted 155 King Street East for rent. I knew I couldn't let this opportunity pass. I sat on a bench in the park across the street and thought my dream could come true. I jumped right into it and signed a lease for 20 years. I didn't think about finances; I just did it. We opened in June 1989 during a full recession but the place was fresh, clean, and new in Toronto. It had outstanding food with a good chef and a good team.

Who was your chef?

BV: My chef was Giampiero Tondina, a Piemontese 'DOC.' He was a really good chef and we started this adventure. I spent all the money that we made. I didn't know what to put on the walls so I put some pictures of the old city and they are still there. I only had enough money for two cases of wine on the first day. Today we have close to 7000 bottles. I worked hard and the place is still going well. I wanted something that spoke for itself and this building was perfect.

Was this area as busy as it is today?

BV: No, people thought I was crazy to come to this area! Jarvis was full of garbage; it was not a nice place to be. But slowly, there were changes. St. James' Cathedral helped to build up this beautiful park in front of the restaurant. New developments came. King Street started to fill up nicely. Now it is clean all the way to the Don Valley Expressway.

Since you opened, how many chefs have you had?

BV: Two.

Who was your second chef?

BV: He was Tommaso Lepore. He's from Campania.

So, he was born and raised in Italy?

BV: Yes, but he also lived in London before he came to Toronto.

Both of your chefs were Italian. Is this a must for you?

BV: Yes, it is. If you want to have an Italian restaurant, the chef should be Italian. I know it's changing. They put a lot of different people in the kitchen, they prepare and pre-cook things beforehand, but I am very traditional and conservative. I want to teach people how to eat and how to do

things. I've been happy and fortunate to have about sixty percent of my staff be Italian. I don't want to discriminate against anybody. Today, everyone becomes a chef within two years. This is not how it should be. They need to have experience. This is what I look for. A chef has to prepare his own menu and then present it to me. A chef has to get a feel for the place. I've been here for fifty years.

A restaurant needs to be taken seriously. It's like a new baby. You need to change diapers. If you neglect customers, eventually you will pay for it. Without the right service, the right ingredients, or if customers order something and you give them something else, they won't come back. Everybody has to be engaged to do a good job.

Biagio has a very classic style, your tables have white tablecloths. You would be classified as fine dining. When people think of Italy they think of the trattoria or the pizzeria, more casual places. How does fine dining co-exist with this idea of Italian dining?

BV: Let's not forget that a good restaurant is still classy with white tablecloths. In a trattoria, everything is family-style and the family makes it. Fine dining is a different thing. I decided to go the fine dining way and I suppose my experiences in London shaped my decision. There I learned what kinds of forks and knives to use. You dress up to come to my restaurant. You don't dress up to go to a trattoria. I would personally not eat in a restaurant where there are no tablecloths because you can eat germs or chemicals that are sprayed. We change our tablecloths all the time. This building will not allow me to become a trattoria. There are a lot of fine dining rooms in Italy, especially in the northern parts, in Milano, Torino, or Verona.

If you want to spend three or four hours with friends, you come to a fine dining restaurant to enjoy good wine and good food. I believe fine dining rooms will come back eventually, even though it is tough moment for them. This place has lasted in Toronto for twenty-four years because we have continuity and we are consistent. We don't change our menu very often. It's a rich menu. A lot of restaurants come and go.

How do you think Italian food will evolve in this country and how has it progressed over the years?

BV: Unfortunately, people see Italian food as pizza, spaghetti, lasagna and meatballs. A few of us have tried to change this style. Since Canadians in general have started to travel, especially to

Italy, I've seen an improvement. People will ask for certain ingredients like arugula, mozzarella di bufala, or burrata. People have more sophisticated tastes. Italian wine is number one in this country; ten years ago it was different. Now people have more education. When I arrived in 1965 no one had heard of parmigiano or gorgonzola but now it is on the mouths of everybody. People have appreciated these beautiful products. The government in Italy, if we ever get one, needs to do more to promote these Italian products. They benefit and we benefit.

Do you feel that promoting Italy is part of your restaurant's mission?

BV: I think all good Italian restaurants are ambassadors. We are the first step in introducing Italian food and culture to Canadians.

You talked about how important it is to have an Italian chef and an Italian staff. What about your ingredients?

BV: Most are local but now we have the luxury of importing prosciutto and salami from Italy. Our cheeses, pasta, and oil are all Italian. I would say it's half and half. It's essential. If you put extra virgin olive oil it has to be Italian.

You're from the south of Italy.

BV: I'm Calabrese.

Did you incorporate that into your identity when you opened the restaurant?

BV: No.

Why not?

BV: I was too young, I had a different mentality. London was like salt and pepper and it changed me a lot. I occasionally worked in an exclusive private men's club. Seeing all these lords come in dressed in coattails and top hats and being served with white gloves shaped me a lot. Where would I have seen that in Calabria? I learned a lot from those old lords. Slowly, I started to appreciate their way of living. They were snobs, but so what? Why open a classy restaurant and add a Calabrese idea? It didn't make sense to me. We do a lot of southern dishes though.

So you learned a lot from this old English tradition …

BV: Oh yes. You have no idea how it transformed me. I have this picture of myself standing in front of a wedding cake with coattails, white gloves, spotless, a shirt with a stiff collar … As you can see, I'm not the typical Calabrese. They changed me for the better but my mentality is still Calabrese.

Is there anything in the Calabrese culture that the English culture lacks?

BV: We are special. We have 'la furbizia.' We are street boys. We know how to survive. My kids are good boys, they try to keep Italian traditions, but they are not street boys. They are not Calabrese. From Campania on down we are a little more 'furbi.' If we don't know something we never say we don't know it; we find a way to get around it. We know how to improvise. The way of living in the north and south of Italy is different. No one can beat a Neapolitan. They are living their life. They live through real life.

Sunday we went out. My daughter is buying a new house in Newcastle. My wife insisted that we go to a pub. She had curried chicken. The next night I took a breast of chicken and said I was going to fix what I didn't like the night before. I started cutting vegetables and mangoes and I made the best meat dish ever. I don't want to generalize but there is something about us in the south that makes us different.

When we were young we didn't have a lot to eat, but we survived. When I went to Switzerland it was tough, but I kept working to make money for my family.

Do you think the new generation of Italian-Canadians has what it takes to create a good Italian restaurant and to transmit the culture?

BV: Unless the parents have the guts to send their kids to Italy for some time and to explore what it is to be Italian, no. Here, our kids are spoiled. We suffered so we don't want our kids to suffer. Sometimes I get mad at myself for it too. Suffering is not a pain, it helps you develop. All Italian kids are spoiled; at eighteen years old they buy a Ferrari. I didn't buy one for my son but some kids have them. When he finished university and started working he bought himself an Alfa Romeo. I didn't object because it was his money. He runs a catering service and is a good boy, and while he would be able to, he doesn't have the guts to run this restaurant. He is serving pasta salad to banks and lawyers; he is imitating Italian food. He has a good business going but it is not what I would like him to do. I wanted him to take over. Unless Italian boys sacrifice themselves and take a few European tours or work in different restaurants I don't think they will be able to open a restaurant the way that I did. To be Italian, I think you have to be born in Italy. You can call yourself Italian because you have Italian parents but you are not Italian.

Your generation arrived here and wanted to cling to Italian traditions and culture because it defined you, but those who were born here wanted to be part of the community around them.

BV: That's right. We don't have to be 100% Italian, but if we're Italian, it's our duty to be Italian. If I wanted to go and speak Italian today where would I go besides College Street? We don't have a centre like we used to. You would go to play cards, have an espresso, meet people, or drink a beer. You exchange ideas. That's why I think it's going to disappear.

CAFÉ DIPLOMATICO
594 College St.

Owner: Rocco Mastrangelo

Opened: 1968

Highlights: espresso, pizza, pitchers of beer, breakfast, anniversary party featuring live music, food, and prizes.

Fact: A section of the menu headed "Alla Canadese" signals the merging of two cultures. Offering hamburgers and grilled cheese alongside veal scaloppini, the 'Dip' serves Italian-Canadian cuisine. At the first hint of summer sun, lineups form for a seat on the sunniest and biggest patio in Little Italy. Look for the Dip in Atom Egoyan's 2009 film *Chloe*, starring Liam Neeson, Julianne Moore and Amanda Seyfried.

Photo: Rocco Mastrangelo

BUCA OSTERIA & ENOTECA

an interview with Robert Gentile

Where does your passion for cooking come from?

RG: I was introduced to food and ingredients and smells at a very young age. My mom, who was a single mom raising me, would drop me off at my grandmother's on her way to work and she would take care of me. Every single day of my childhood for however many years, had something to do with food. It didn't matter the time of the year. I was always being fed or around food. In the summer, we would be in the garden. At other times we would make gnocchi. It would get to the point where I would ask to watch cooking shows on TV. My grandmother thought it was crazy that I wanted to watch those and not cartoons. That was embedded in my head at a young age. I was especially exposed to that because I spent so much time with my grandmother.

I'm assuming she was a great cook?

RG: Yes.

Which region was she from?

RG: She was *ciociara*, so from Lazio. The other half of my family is from Abruzzo. Even just waking up in the morning there was always something to smell. It could be the smell of brodo or tomato sauce. My close relationship with my grandmother defined my passion. It was something I enjoyed and it was so interesting to me that something from the garden or the store could be transformed into something incredible.

When did you realize food was more than just a hobby or a pleasure?

RG: There came a point in my life where, yes, I loved food and making myself lunch and cooking shows, but then, of course, I also wanted things. And the things that I wanted required money. My mother basically turned to me and said, "I'm not going to give you money for the rest of your life. If you want things you need to go to work." I was about thirteen years old. She told me that I needed to find something that I truly enjoyed because I would be doing it for the rest of my life. I never thought of it like that. At that age, the thought of doing something for the rest of my life that I didn't like sucked. I immediately started thinking about which things having to do with food would make me money. One of the things that came up was becoming a chef. At that age I decided to try it out and see what would happen. My mom knew someone through the church that owned a restaurant and she brought me there to go to work. I interviewed with the chef and she took me.

What did you do?

RG: I was a dishwasher. Every so often I would sneak into the kitchen and observe and ask if there was something I could do, even if it was just chopping parsley or potatoes.

Was it an Italian restaurant?

RG: Yes. Those kinds of things led me down this path. I mean, when you tell someone you enjoy chopping parsley, they think you're nuts, but I enjoyed it.

Did you ever go to culinary school?

RG: During high school I bounced around a lot of different restaurants where I grew up. Some were Italian restaurants, others were diners. I made a lot of friends that also liked to cook and that's what we did. I got a job here and there, but then high school was up. My parents wanted me to go to university but school wasn't my thing and I didn't want to go. I was very anxious. I was always 'go, go, go' and sitting in a classroom reading off a chalkboard was not for me. I had to be involved with things in a creative way. After high school I decided I wasn't going to university and that I was going to be a chef. Everyone thought that was outrageous and that I was crazy.

Your parents were shocked?

RG: Completely against it, but the thought of me having to go to university was just …

You had to fight for it?

RG: Yes, I definitely had to put my foot down. I went to George Brown College when I was eighteen. I did one year there. It was an interesting experience. The school was going through a transitional period where they were getting out of the old-school way of teaching culinary skills and moving more into the direction of where they are now, which is an institute. I felt after one year that, while my experience wasn't totally horrible, I could learn a lot more just by going to work. Right after my year at George Brown I started with Chef McEwan. I was nineteen years old. I started at North 44.

You started in the kitchen? Cooking?

RG: Yes, it was entry level. I worked twelve hours per day in a serious professional environment.

Is that where you learned technique?

RG: Absolutely. It defined my career.

When did you open Buca? And how did you know you were ready to have your own place and your own menu?

RG: Well, I was with Chef McEwan for ten years. A lot of time had passed and I was comfortable. There was a lot going on in McEwan's company. I had moved from North 44 to Bymark to One in Yorkville. One year and a half into opening One there were rumours that another Italian restaurant was going to open—what would be Fabbrica. I got to a point in my career where the decisions I wanted to make were beyond my position. I wanted to tell the managers what to do, and just wanted to do more. I started to get an itch and being in a situation like that wasn't good enough for me anymore.

Were you still cooking Italian?

RG: Chef McEwan has a lot of Italian influence on his menus and he is a huge fan of Italian food, but there was also a huge French and Asian influence everywhere. It got to a point where I just wanted to see what was out there and what other options I had.

I started making connections and it's funny how the universe brings you what you want. People I didn't even know started calling because they had heard that I was potentially going to open my own restaurant. One of my good friends who I had worked with at Grazie when I was eighteen told me he was going to open a French bistro. He said I was welcome to come and take a look at it because he was looking for a chef. I looked at it and thought, "That isn't my thing." I needed to find something a little bit more in my heart. After I turned that down, he said that he knew a couple of guys who had a space and they wanted to open up an Italian restaurant but they needed a chef. He said once I saw the space I was going to freak out. He connected me with Peter and Gus, who are now my partners. I met with them and we had a casual conversation about Italian food and we just hit it off. They brought me over here to see this space and once I saw it, I said, "Wow!" It was special and it immediately meant something to me. It was a tough decision to leave Chef McEwan. It was October 2009 and the stock market had just crashed. The whole world was on fire and no one was even remotely thinking of opening up a restaurant. Even my family members were telling me I was crazy to leave a chef who was so well-established and paying me well. There was a lot of tugging. You have to take a risk in life and it hit me that this was the right decision.

Let's talk about risk and the menu at Buca. It's not what you immediately think of as Italian. It's sophisticated and creative. Did you dream of this menu from the start and did you have to walk your clients through it?

RG: There was definitely a process. We wanted to make sure that we portrayed the seriousness of what we considered to be Italian cuisine. It wasn't a place to get veal parmigiana. Even if we did make veal parmigiana, we wanted to do it in a way that put an authentic spin on the dish.

So you wanted to revisit something traditional?

RG: Absolutely. What we do is travel a lot to Italy and source out. Every region of Italy has its own specialty. There are so many specifics everywhere you go. Every time I go into a different region of Italy there is something that no one even knows about. Even within each region there are towns that do their own thing. For example, we have melanzane al cioccolato on the dessert menu. It's a dish I learned to make from somebody's grandmother in Amalfi. We went through it step-by-step. But that's a dessert that belongs to Campania where they make dessert with eggplant. We took that recipe back to Canada and thought about the ingredients we have here. We flew in the spices to make the Concerto, which is a liquor similar to a Jagermeister. It's black and there's orzo in it. That liquor took us three and a half months to make and this is before we can even get started on the dish. If you go to a pharmacy in Amalfi you can buy 98% alcohol and the spices you need and just go home and make the Concerto. Here you can't get 98% alcohol. We sourced alcohol from Quebec that was 95% proof. We brought it here. I got my friend who was in Amalfi to bring back 10 to 15 packets of those spices. Each packet makes four litres of alcohol. We flew it here and put it together. Then we said these are the ingredients that make melanzane al cioccolato: orange, eggplant, amaretti, dulce de leche, chocolate, and Concerto. They make it like a big lasagna but we were thinking about how we could make it like a professional chef's refined dish.

When you opened Buca did you think the public was ready for this type of cuisine?

RG: Let me give you an example: lamb's brain alla saltimbocca: it's been on the menu since day one. You have salty pork, strong sage, and creamy lamb's brain. Lamb's brain has an intense flavour: it's lamb, but it's in your face. We also had pig's ears and salumi—with the legs hanging—on the menu when we first opened as well. We're not trying to say, "Look how cool we are. We have lamb's brain on the menu." We're trying to be authentic. We're not going to do things that Italy wouldn't do. All of these things on our menu are things that I've either seen there, I've eaten there, somebody's nonna has made for me, or somebody has brought me back from there. One guy brought me back fermented ricotta which was one hundred days old, and we now make that here. Our red wine vinegar is in a barrel in the back and it is the vinegar my family started here thirty-two years ago when they arrived. Real balsamic vinegar is stuff that is aged in barrels and takes a minimum of fifteen years and a lot of money to get right. So they use wine vinegar because they make the vinegar when they make the wine. So the lamb's brain and the pig's ears and the torta al sanguinaccio or the gelato we make with pig's blood are not on our menu because we're trying to be cool. This is what they eat in Italy. It doesn't matter if it's the pig's foot or tongue or ears, Italians will use it up, but they're using it up because it's good.

While it's true you are creating something authentic and traditional, I can't help but think that it's more complex in terms of preparation than Italian food you might get somewhere else. So there is a level of sophistication that the individual should be able to appreciate. How do you do that while balancing it with the perceived simplicity of Italian food?

RG: My take on that is that simplicity and ingredients are number one. Our effort in sourcing the best ingredients is the number one priority of the restaurant. When we have a menu meeting, we

have lists of all of the ingredients in season, organized by month. A week ago, my chefs and I met on Sunday afternoon with some coffee and some cookbooks. We look at our list of seasonal ingredients and, since we are now in March, we'll need to have a menu full of spring menu items until May. Something like nettles are only in specific areas of Italy because they can only grow in certain areas. We have the ability to say we're doing Tuscan cuisine or we're doing Sicilian cuisine because Ontario is very different from Italy in terms of what we can get.

So is being in Ontario an advantage?

RG: It's not that we have more. Here someone could ask you what kind of Italian cuisine you're cooking and there is nothing specific. But if I was in Sicily and someone asked me the same question, well, I would be doing Sicilian dishes because of the ingredients I'm getting. Here I could get things that are Sicilian and things that are Northern Italian because we're in Ontario, so it starts with the ingredients.

From there, we take a professional chef's approach to making torta al sanguinaccio or melanzane al cioccolato. Take the melanzane alla parmigiana—professional chef's approach means you take the ricotta, which comes in each day fresh and warm, and whip it. We cut the eggplant so that they're in perfect little rings, and then we use a piping bag to layer the tomato and ricotta before putting the burrata on top. We take the presentation to another level. We have all sorts of equipment and training that we implement. We inject a professional chef's take into something nonna would do, but at the end of the day it's still fried eggplant, ricotta cheese, and tomato.

Another example is the stuffed calamari. Nonna would make the stuffed calamari by putting them in a roasting pan with some tomatoes and bay leaves and throw them in the oven. Here, we vacuum pack them individually, cook them in a water bath, and they take on a texture that you would normally not get if you just threw them in an oven for an hour. So we have some pieces of equipment that nonna wouldn't have at home. We want to take the dining experience to another level for our customers. At the end of the day, the focus on the food and the experience of the customers is our main priority.

How do you adapt offering customers a great food experience to the North American hurried pace?

RG: Well, in Italy restaurants are open for two or maybe three hours. That's it. They're not in the business of 'go, go, go' like in North America. Here you have a standardized breakdown of how a restaurant works: you have two seatings. You give yourself blocks of time when customers are seated. We give customer two and a half to three hours for dinner. Every once and a while you get the odd group that wants to make a night of it. You have to work around that kind of thing. Our tasting menu is designed to get you in and out within two and a half hours.

Do you think that your understanding of Italian food is something that many Italian-Canadians of your generation also have? Has culture changed their understanding of it?

RG: It's starting to really open people's minds. We get a lot of people from Italy here and they think 'wow' because many of these things are familiar to them. But then we get a lot of Italian-Canadians that have never seen any of this and they have the same reaction of 'wow.' Buca is not a place for dishes that everybody knows. We don't want to make people uncomfortable. We want people to come here and try things they have never experienced.

What is it that makes you stay in the restaurant business when the city is full of Italian restaurants?

RG: I think we have something very special here. We have a restaurant that is consistently busy. We've hit a niche concept. We're a little bit special in the fact that we have all of these interesting things and take them to the next level. We're not trying to be safe. We have a great brand and reputation as well and we want to expand on that. We have plans to do a trattoria concept or a Bar Buca. We have a Yorkville Buca which will be different from the King Street Buca. We have ideas of opening up a pasticceria or a pizzeria, so there are a lot of different things we can do.

Do you still have the time to go into the kitchen and cook or do you just direct the menu meetings?

RG: I do, but it depends. My work goes in waves. Right now, I'm working a lot on the new project and we also have another restaurant, The Saint, on Ossington. Right now I'm working on Bar Buca which should be open in May.

Where will it be?

RG: Just down the street on Portland. It's our Italian bar concept. Anyone who's very familiar with Italy knows that when you wake up in the morning you go to the bar for a coffee and a dolce or a cornetto. For lunch, you might go for a panino and a glass of wine. At night you can go and have an aperitivo and hang out. In Italy the café is a neighbourhood hub where you can go and have anything you want. That's what our bar concept is going to be. Everyone thinks it's going to be a nightclub because it's 'Bar' Buca. Again, it's more education. We're not a nightclub or a bar where we're going to have people partying. It's an Italian concept we're trying to inject into our way of life in North America.

Which ingredient is revolutionary or fundamental to you?

RG: I don't know if they're revolutionary, but my favourite thing to work with is tomatoes. I can drink tomato sauce. For me there is nothing better than tomato sauce made from the bushels and the smell of the boiled tomatoes. I get emotional thinking about it. Eating that with pasta is the greatest thing in the world to me. I'll take it over chocolate cake and ice cream any day. Even the addition of tomato sauce to dishes here and there adds an incredible flavour. A fresh, raw tomato is so perfect.

Where do you get your tomatoes?

RG: At Buca we use Cookstown Greens. They have some of the best tomatoes I've ever tried. We don't put tomatoes on the menu until they're in season. When they are in season we'll make bushels of sauce and have them all in jars. We'll have pasta al pomodoro on the menu only when tomatoes are in season. If not, you won't see it. The second ingredient is eggs. Fowl eggs, duck eggs, quail eggs, chicken eggs ... you name them, I love them all. They're so versatile and you can do so many different things with the egg yolk specifically. Whether you poach it or fry it or make a dressing with it, your options are endless.

You put egg yolks on pizza, right?

RG: Yes. We put them on pizza and pour them on risotto. You can just put them in a mixing bowl and add icing sugar to them. My grandmother would give me raw egg yolks with sugar and espresso to shut me up as a kid. I would eat it with a spoon.

What is your favourite or signature dish?

RG: My personal favourite? There are a lots of them. I'm very drawn to the spaghetti al nero di maiale and the lamb's brain too. It's special in the fact that we make the pasta with just pork blood. There's no addition of eggs, flour, or water. The combination of flavours in that dish is so intense that you hit all the levels of 'umami.' You have spice, smoky flavour, cured 'nduja, the bitter taste of the rapini and the salty flavour. It's a very versatile dish. We'll do it with radicchio in the fall instead of rapini. You change the bitter aspect of it and it's an awesome dish.

Your chef is not Italian. Do you both go to Italy or do you go alone?

RG: He's a trained soldier of Italy. He trained under me, went to Italy and worked for the Santini family at a three-star Michelin restaurant in Mantova, and also worked in Rome. Now he's back again and will be the chef de cuisine at the Buca location in Yorkville. The chef de cuisine at this King Street location is Korean. He's a trained soldier of Italian cuisine as well.

So there is a place for non-Italians in traditional Italian cuisine?

RG: Absolutely. Yong has been with me since he first held a knife and now he's the head chef. If anyone knows Italian cuisine it's Yong. He's been here for four years. It's drilled in his head. He knows what Buca is and he knows how to come up with really cool things.

CALIFORNIA SANDWICHES

10 Locations in Toronto, Mississauga, Etobicoke, Woodbridge, Richmond Hill, and Scarborough

Owners: Papa-Bertucci family

Opened: 1967

Originally: La Rinascente Grocery

Menu highlights: Veal Cutlet Sandwich

Awards: Best Italian Sandwich: *Toronto Life*, *Now Magazine* Best of Toronto, *Toronto Sun* Readers' Choice Awards

Fact: The original location was a closely guarded secret for years; regulars selectively initiated new customers into the sect-like devotion to this sandwich. In the first year La Rinascente opened, the first batch of breaded veal cutlets, ladled with homemade sauce, and sweet peppers on a fresh bun, were served. The iconic sandwich launched the new business that would replace the grocery store and led to the ever-expanding universe that is California Sandwiches.

Photos courtesy of California Sandwiches and Deborah Verginella

CAMPAGNOLO

an interview with Craig Harding

When did you open Campagnolo?

CH: We opened in November 2010.

And in 2011 you were voted one of the best restaurants?

CH: Right. enRoute magazine, which is one of Air Canada's publications, listed us as one of the top ten new restaurants in 2011. In 2012, Maclean's did an issue on the top fifty restaurants to eat at now in Canada and we made the top fifty. We've been on the famous food critic, Joanne Kates's list. We've been very fortunate to get a lot of great reviews.

Your name is not Italian.

CH: No. I come from a European background. My father has German and English in his blood, but my mother was born in Italy. She came from Toritto with her two parents. One was a miner and one was a seamstress. They came to Canada in the 1960s for the opportunities and for a job for my nonno, who was a miner. They lived in Sudbury and in Kirkland Lake. My grandparents spent five or six years up north before moving to Toronto for more opportunities. I also always had a larger family on my Italian side, so even though my name is not Italian, I feel like I embody a lot of the characteristics and passions of that side. I feel very Italian more than anything. We're all Canadian but I cherish that Italian side because it has given me a lot of inspiration in my career and I love that. I've always loved food, eating, family, and entertaining. That I made a decision to go in that direction is something that I owe to my grandparents, and it has been a big inspiration.

What are some of those Italian characteristics?

CH: I think a lot of cultures are like this, but I know Italians love to socialize around the dinner table. When your friends come over and even if they're not Italian, you always go into the kitchen and bring out some food. Italians are very food-oriented and passionate about the quality things and eating with people they love. They're very generous with their time and with what they have. When my parents split up I spent a lot of time at my nonna's house. I was the first of the grandkids. I was fortunate enough to get her at a young age when she was still very active. She had a lot of friends that would come in and out and bring food and laugh. We celebrated every single birthday of all my family members. There would be tons of food and I always looked forward to the next get-together. I always wanted to know what we were going to be eating. Then I started to help her cook. I loved the gratification of giving someone a nice meal and making them so happy. I wanted to create that all the time, every day.

When did you decide to make this a career?

CH: Well, it was near the end of high school when you have to make a decision about what you want to do. It wasn't that I didn't do well academically, I just wasn't interested in any one area enough or have the passion for anything to study it the next year in university. I knew I would not make the most of it. I think you really have to be invested in something to get the most of your education, so I decided to change schools. My last year of high school I switched to a technical school in Toronto. I guess I should also mention that my mom had divorced my dad and married a man from Newfoundland who had a house in Woodbridge before the subdivisions were even built. I was living there, and as you know, Woodbridge is a very Italian area so all of my friends and the people I grew up with were Italian. My dad lived in the city and I thought that there were so many cool things happening

in the city so I moved to Toronto in the west end. There was a program at Central Tech that had a cooking class. I thought I would go there and try cooking full-time. I happened to get a teacher who was a Swiss chef that worked in all of the top hotels in Europe. He wasn't just a Home Economics teacher teaching cooking. When I was there, he saw that I was interested more than the other students in the classroom who just took it for an easy credit; he took me under his wing and showed me a few things. I really enjoyed that, so I applied to the George Brown Culinary Management program and the following September, I went. The rest is history, I guess. I started working and meeting people …

What did you do after you graduated?

CH: From the time that I graduated to the time that I opened was about ten years. During that time, I worked in other kitchens and travelled. I travelled to Australia for eight months, as well as to Europe and Southeast Asia. I was working in Australia. I went to Italy a few times. Now I try to go to Italy every year. It was all of those experiences that helped me decide to do this. I always knew that I wanted to be my own boss but it took me awhile to decide to do this. I met a woman, now my fiancée Alexandra, who came into the picture in 2007. She was a server at a restaurant as well as an interior designer. In 2009 when we decided we were going to open a restaurant, we left Toronto to go to British Columbia. We were going to try living in another place in Canada and see something new but we didn't quite like it out there, so we decided to come back. Together, we thought about the concept of this restaurant. So, still in 2009, we moved back to Toronto and moved in with my nonna. It was very nice for her because she was alone and loved having the company. I was able to reconnect with that type of cooking and eating. Alex and I decided it was going to be a very simple and rustic place with Italian roots, but that sometimes we could do

something different because I'm a trained chef and know French. The idea was that it would be farm to table, and that's how we came up with the name Campagnolo. I was talking with my nonna and I said, "What do you think of when I say farm to table?" She said, "Contadino." But I thought that was too hard. I didn't even necessarily want an Italian name, but when she said "campagnolo" I loved it. I liked the idea of being in the country and a lot of my nonna's friends had farms, with chickens, that we used to go to. It felt rural. It was very interesting. I really liked that whole idea.

Tell me about your menu, and the way you cook, and how the French techniques influence your Italian bent.

CH: I guess there's been a bit of an evolution. In the beginning, our menu was very small. Not that it's big today, but it was very rustic. There were simple pastas, simple meats. Artichokes might have been one dish. As the team has grown, we've improved the kitchen size and put a little bit more thought into some of the dishes. What I really like about the menu now is that there's an element of surprise. One dish might be a simple lasagna. One might be a ragù with tripe, polenta, wild boar, etc. That stuff is all very rustic. Another dish might be more complicated, like beef carpaccio with Dungeness crab and black truffles and wild mushrooms presented beautifully on a large plate. So one dish might be very simple, and another might be very complicated, but as long as it tastes good and as long as the dishes don't come across as too intricate or over the top, that's what matters. We have such a great group of guys here, so we collaborate a lot. We cook with what's in season and with what we have. We talk about things we've seen at the market, what's fresh, and what's good to cook with now. Because we change the menu every day, we have to come up with new dishes all the time.

You change the whole menu every day?

CH: If the menu has fourteen things on it, five of them are always there. The other nine things we change all the time. This week we're doing three new dishes and last week we had three dishes that we're not doing anymore. Next week we might do two new dishes and get rid of two more. It's a couple in and a couple out. We don't switch everything all at once. It would be too much work and too complicated.

Is this what it takes to keep clients happy in Toronto where people are more and more knowledgeable about what is authentically Italian?

CH: That's part of it. It's about maintaining a balance between the quality, the price, and your expectations. On my days off, I go to places like Pizzeria Libretto because it's cheap and I know what I'm getting, but sometimes I eat there and I think that, even though it's good, I'm eating the same old boring arugula salad with pears. Here, there are dishes that we will always have, but then there are new dishes, and as long as those new dishes are as high quality as the other dishes, that's good. They know they can come and get spaghetti all'amatriciana and a few other things. But, because there is familiarity and there is always something new, people feel comfortable and they trust us. They come back. I think some people want really authentic stuff and others want to try something completely new. As long as it's done well, then I think we've done our job.

Are you creating a new interpretation of Italian food? You're not necessarily cooking traditional dishes.

CH: Not always. Sometimes, yes. But sometimes I'll get an ingredient like puntarelle and I want to make them the way they do in Rome with anchovies, anchovy dressing, oil, and vinegar. It's the same thing with spaghetti all'amatriciana. I don't want to mess with it. But then there are some dishes that I'll put a spin on.

Can you give me an example?

CH: Sure. Let's use chicken cacciatore as an example. It's very open to interpretation. We make it with a restaurant-type interpretation. Instead of just cooking the whole bird or chopping it up in a pan, we debone the entire bird, stuff the legs, cut them into perfectly round shapes, and cook them in a water bath, which is a more modern technique. One week we might have a dish that is very rustic, and the next week we'll cook something that is more three star Michelin and refined. And both of those dishes are at the same restaurant. It depends on what we feel like. We don't want to do it all in one direction either way.

Which ingredients are imported?

CH: The pasta and a lot of the cheeses are imported. The fresh cheeses like mozzarella and burrata you can buy here. Everything is fresh here, which is great. I buy the aged cheeses from Italy. I import olive oil, but also certain produce like artichokes and lettuce. Being from the north, I love the bitter greens and will bring in the radicchio di Treviso and the puntarelle. It's very expensive. Sometimes I'll get apples or oranges as well.

Is your menu inspired from the north or the south of Italy?

CH: Everything. There's so much. I don't want to do just one dish. I want to do swordfish with pine nuts and anchovies like in Sicily, and all of the great dishes in Tuscany and the north. I mix it up.

What distinguishes Campagnolo in a city full of Italian restaurants? What makes you competitive?

CH: I think I understand hospitality. A lot of people can cook, but when you have a whole restaurant committed to the attitude of making people happy, that makes a difference. We have an open kitchen so sometimes I can come out and talk to people. It's very small and I want to make sure that people are happy about the food, the price, the temperature of the wine, the service, the lighting, and the sound. If all of that's right, I think you will be successful.

Why did you choose Dundas Street West?

CH: It was cheap and it was a corner with patio potential. When it's your first business, and you don't have a lot of money, and are risking everything, you don't want to spend a lot. At least if it doesn't do well, the rent is cheap.

So, are you a destination restaurant or a neighbourhood restaurant?

CH: Probably more destination, for sure. Of course, there are people in the neighbourhood that come, but people are coming from all over.

Do you see any up-and-coming trends in Italian food?

CH: I don't know, but I've seen a lot of my friends open restaurants and they do so well. I think all nationalities across Toronto love Italian food. I look at all of the Italian restaurants out there and they're always busy. Italian food is a sure bet because it's fun, it's for every day of the week, it's not too fancy, and people like it. I think it's going to grow. Ten years ago people thought Italian food was tomato cream sauce. It was shit. When I learned how to cook and worked at places like Il Fornello, it was terrible. Now people want authentic. Today, if you don't make fresh pasta, forget about it, because everyone else is making fresh pasta and fresh bread and their own salami. The level and quality of products and the sourcing is only going to get better. I was thinking of opening up a restaurant that served only pasta. There would be ten to twelve pasta dishes and everything would be fresh everyday. Where do you get that? No one has done that yet. Ten years ago you would never think of that. People think they can just get away with De Cecco penne, but that's not really Italian. That's what you cook at home when you're in a rush.

COPPI

an interview with Alessandro Scotto

What year did you open?

AS: The restaurant opened in 1991 in the middle of a recession. The idea was to keep things very simple. By that I mean that the dishes on the menu would highlight things considered to be traditionally Italian and not regional. We had certain philosophies and one of the philosophies was to never be heavy, so we stayed away from northern-style dishes. That turned out to be quite a plus because it went hand-in-hand with the 'healthy food' revolution. I think that had a lot to do with our success. That was our blueprint from the get-go.

Why did you choose the Lawrence Park area as the location for your restaurant?

AS: It's affluent. People understand the cuisine and they also understand and appreciate fine dining ... although, now the fine dining experience has very much changed.... As you can see, we don't even have linens anymore. But, at the time, that type of experience was what people wanted and expected.

Let's talk about the linens. Was that a conscious choice?

AS: Yes, absolutely. We think that nowadays the whole silverware, linen, and waiter with a tie is something that we're moving away from because the focus is on what's on the plate. People are more interested in the food. You can get away with a lot less these days and so the standard is very high. With that came the focus on the food as opposed to all of the other aspects of the restaurant, which are very minimal.

Where are you from?

AS: I'm from Napoli, my chef is from the Puglia region, and my ex-partner was from Abruzzi. We always thought that we wanted to showcase a certain diet that influenced our way of eating and one we thought highly of.

Is it difficult to sustain this type of menu with the climate here and the availability of ingredients?

AS: That's a challenge. Nowadays, we can get just about anything in the world. So that's one of the good

things. One of the bad things is that we assume that tomatoes are going to be good all year. So there are good and bad things. Once upon a time, we used to get the produce only when it was in season, but now we see it all the time. It's a challenge to know what to use and when to use it. We've always tried to stay focused on not so many ingredients and using the ones that will bring the best flavours to the mouth.

Do you change the menu accordingly?

AS: We do and we don't. What we like to do is change the sides, the vegetables, and the pastas now and again. We change our specials. The fish special is really important to us because a lot of people come here for fish and it brings in a lot of sales. We're always careful about where we're buying it from and if it's sustainable or on the endangered list. That's always been very important to us. On the menu, we have a sea bream and a sea bass from Italy and we make sure it's farmed fish. Back in the day, everyone wanted wild fish, but now they're moving away from that. We want sustainable farming practices and that's what we're looking for. I heard they're doing it in Italy, but also in Spain and Greece as well. I think that's the future of our industry.

You talked about your chef and your ex-partner both being Italian. Do you think it's possible to create something authentically Italian being Italian-Canadian or do you think you need to be Italian?

AS: No, I don't think so anymore. You don't have to be. Italian food has transcended cultural boundaries. I've had some very good Italian food prepared by Sri Lankan chefs that was just incredible. A classic dish like spaghetti and meatballs, for example, is more an American dish than it is an Italian dish. The pizza that they make in Chicago is American. I think Italian food has inspired the world.

So you can have a different version of Italian food?

AS: Absolutely. There are no rules. We may tell a client not to put cheese on that seafood dish, but not because we're trying to tell them that Italians don't eat it that way. We're just trying to say that if you put cheese on the seafood, it will take away from the taste of the seafood, so try it without it first. Chefs try new things every day, and a lot has to do with what is available to them. Who is to say that some things can't come out better here than they do in Italy?

Why did you name your restaurant Coppi?

AS: My ex-partner was named Fausto and his father was a cycling enthusiast. My partner used to tell me stories of his father watching the Giro d'Italia and cheering for Fausto Coppi. So he named the restaurant after him. It all came from his father more than anything. There's no familial relation between him and Fausto Coppi, though that would have been interesting. I think it works for a restaurant. It's short, it sounds Italian, and suggests something old and traditional. It just made sense. I always thought of it as the perfect name.

Is the role of Coppi to preserve Italian culture or offer a new version of it?

AS: I think our role is to create an experience that blends tradition with new ways of preparing these traditional dishes. I really hate to use the word fusion, but it really is a fusion of new and old.

Why do you hate to use that word?

AS: Well, because it suggests the opposite of traditional. When I use the word "fusion" I mean to actually fuse new ideas and what is available to us with traditional ways. We still braise our meats the same way they did years ago, but perhaps they taste a little bit different because we have new cuts and new ingredients as well.

Let's talk about the eating experience. Did you grow up with the Italian idea of eating as ritual?

AS: For sure. Very much so.

Is this something, as a restaurant in North America, you can offer to your clients? Are you limited in terms of the fast-paced lifestyle?

AS: That's a good question because that's something we see less and less of. We used to have salad with the main course but now it's served as an appetizer. There's a lot of sharing of dishes, which is a wonderful thing, but it's changing and evolving. Other little things, like, you don't eat until everyone's at the table, is something that doesn't exist anymore. That's

one of those things that we try to keep wholesome in this restaurant. There's coursing: you have the primo and then the secondo. Not everyone appreciates or knows about that, but we try to maintain it.

Do you need to travel to Italy to get refreshed and inspired?

AS: Yes, we do make a point of it. We do go, but maybe not as often as we'd like. This is the age of the internet, so you can get a lot of information that way as well. You can see what chefs are doing. There's that benefit.

Do you import a lot of ingredients from Italy?

AS: Yes. But we also try to use as many local products as possible. I remember a few years ago I thought, "I wonder if we could do a traditional Italian restaurant without importing?" and the answer is that you just can't. Take a basic ingredient like a tomato, for example. We use the San Marzano tomato, a really good plum tomato from the Napoli region. If you ask my father, he says that the tomatoes he cans himself are as good here as they are in Italy, but they're just not. The San Marzano tomatoes are just the best. And that's not even getting into detail about the cheese. Sure, there are some very good local cheeses, but we can't make mozzarella the way that they do there. It's impossible. The idea of everything local for a good Italian restaurant is, in my opinion, impossible.

What or who inspired you to follow this path?

AS: I wish it came from an inspiration. I grew up in restaurants. My first taste of the restaurant business was when I was really little. We went to Italy and opened up a restaurant in Milan for a couple of years. Then we came back because it was literally tearing our family apart. We collectively decided to come back home. When we came back, we opened up another restaurant. It's a family tradition. It's in me. When I grew up we weren't well off, so school wasn't really in the picture for me. I stuck to this.

Are Italian-Canadians still on top of the business in that sense?

AS: No. It's really tough to run a restaurant right now. It's expensive. This is a foodie city so there's a lot of competition. If we had to bump our costs every time the prices were bumped on us we'd be charging $30.00 for a plate of pasta. If we kept the same profit margins it would be crazy. We have to compromise our profit margins. And then you have to couple that with the recession. Fine dining depends a lot on the expense account and we don't see that anymore. We almost have to rethink the design and functionality of the restaurant. You almost can't offer those high-end dishes anymore. We've tweaked the menu a little bit. I'm not complaining because we have a good reputation. People come here for good food so we do well. I don't think I'd want my kids in this business because it's so tough and so cut-throat. I think a lot of Italians feel the same way. My partner doesn't want his kids in the industry either. If you see Italians in the industry right now, they've either been here for a while like me, or they're young, exceptional chefs who have travelled to Italy. I'm working sixty to seventy hours a week so I can put some money aside for my kids' schooling so they don't have to.

Do you have a signature dish or a personal favourite on your menu?

AS: The signature dish is the fish in the sauce; that, or the risotto. It looks really good because sometimes it comes out of a big wheel of parmigiano, which is awesome, but more importantly, it's the risotto itself. Our kitchen really knows how to prepare a good risotto. Apparently that's hard to get in this city. I know Mistura makes an incredible risotto. So, whether it's the risotto with

porcini mushrooms that comes out of the wheel of parmigiano or the risotto with truffles in the fall, people have come to appreciate our risotto. And then there's the fish with the salt. Apparently it's something that can be seen more and more often now. I've heard that they're preparing it that way in Las Vegas, but for the longest time we were the only restaurant doing it. It's a steamed fish at the end of the day. It's ironic because it's a big production when it's presented and you see this big mound of salt, but it's the simplicity that makes it so special. People have come to appreciate that.

And your favourite?

AS: I'm going to pick the fresh anchovies that we've been doing lately. We've been getting these anchovies from the Mediterranean about twice a month. They bring them in every Thursday and they're really fresh. So we fillet them, clean them, and then sometimes we fry them, or what we like to do is cure them. We let them rest in a red wine vinegar for three to four hours. We press them and dry them, and then we marinate them in garlic, fresh olive oil and pistachio. They're incredible. They're to die for. They're not salty like people expect them to be because they're not canned, but they still have that fattiness that anchovies have. They're full of Omega-3. So, that's my favourite. We also make a very good carpaccio.

How do you make that?

AS: Well, that's one of the chef's secrets. It has to do with the brining process. What he does is let it rest in salted water for a particular amount of time. He dries it and then freezes it. We slice it and add some olive oil, lemon juice, chopped arugula, and some pine nuts. It's very tasty.

Is there anything specific from Napoli that you've incorporated?

AS: I always fight with the chef about this one little thing. We have this beautiful mozzarella di bufala that comes in. The chef likes to reduce balsamic vinegar and he puts it on the side as a dressing. Every time I see that I cringe because balsamic vinegar is a very northern thing. It's very strong, it's very sweet, and it has nothing to do with mozzarella di bufala. But there are so many influences from Napoli on the menu.

Have you seen a difference in trends in this industry since you first opened?

AS: Yes. First of all, I see it in alcohol consumption: people are drinking a lot less. I've also noticed a lot of price-conscious decisions being made when ordering. There's a lot of sharing. There are a lot less expense account dinners. And the actual diet is changing, people are very conscious. That's a plus

for us because we already cook that way. We minimally fry and we use olive oil instead of butter. I see a lot of people appreciating that more. So people are more health-conscious and price-conscious.

What else about Coppi makes it different?

AS: We're really big into cycling. We're really happy that thanks to the Canadian rider winning the Giro d'Italia last year, cycling has been elevated in the national consciousness. That's pretty cool because we've been here twenty-two years and that has been really relevant to us.

We've also been bringing in white truffles from Northern Italy for more than sixteen years. They're the tuber magnatum pico truffle. Very few people knew about truffles when we were getting them initially. You had to be a chef and a European chef to know about them. Back then we were paying $300.00 per kilo which was very high back then. Now we pay upwards of $7000.00 per kilo because the yield hasn't changed much but the demand has gone through the roof.

So the Canadian public is more knowledgeable about things?

AS: Yes. Thanks to travelling, thanks to the Food Network, and things like that. People have caught on. Like I said, this is a foodie city. People come from far to have truffles here. Fifteen or sixteen years ago I doubt many restaurants served truffles, but today many are. Last year I got 5.5 or 6 kilos of truffles which was my highest amount ever. I think Coppi is one of the original restaurants to serve truffles in very traditional ways. We serve them with eggs, with risotto, with carpaccio, with veal, and with the taglierini. The menu doesn't change that much.

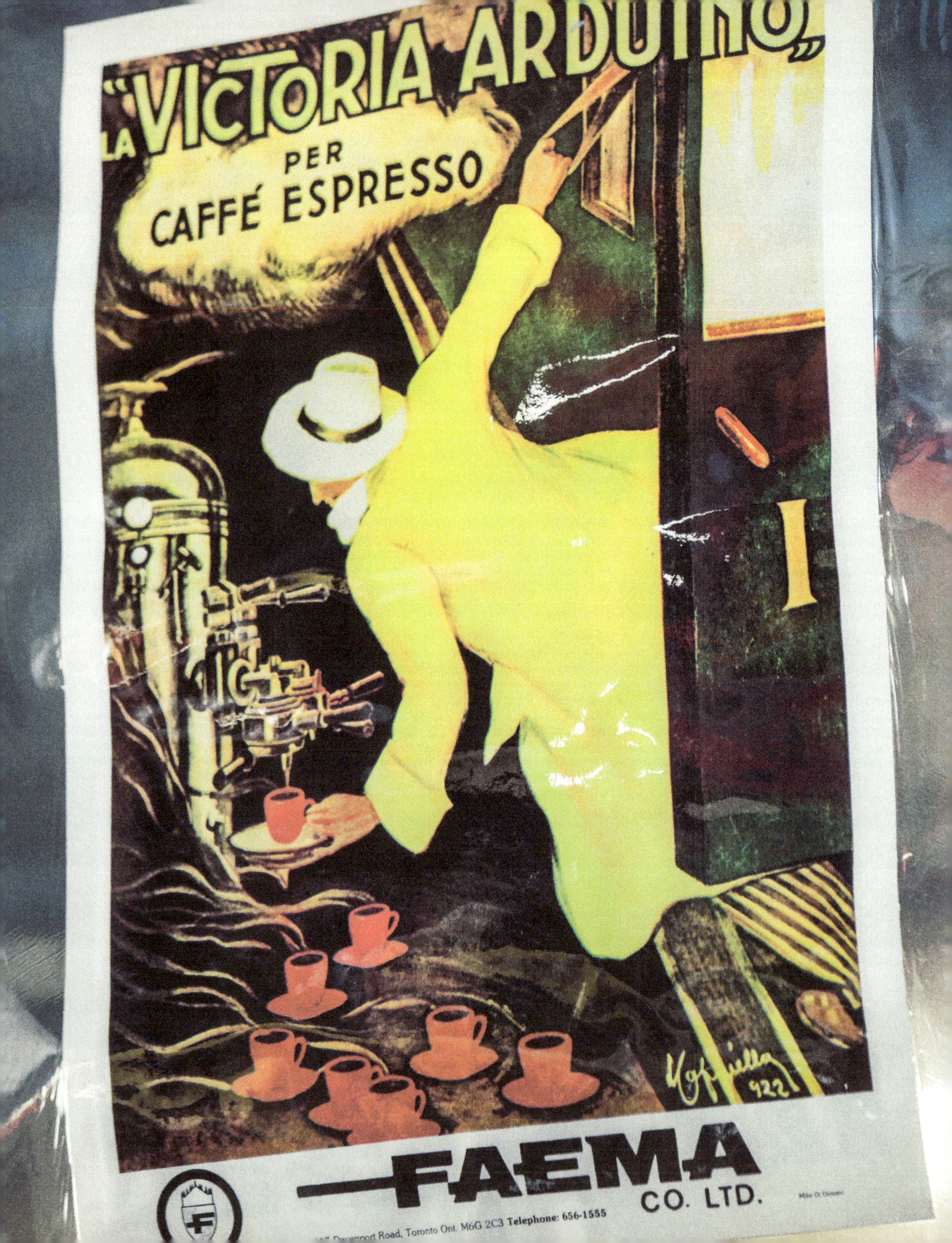

LA "VICTORIA ARDUINO"
PER
CAFFÉ ESPRESSO
FAEMA
CO. LTD.
Road, Toronto Ont. M6G 2C3 Telephone: 656-1555

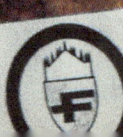

FAEMA

an interview with Mike Di Donato

What were your beginnings in business here?

MD: I came to Canada in November 1956. I went from Napoli to New York and then from New York to Toronto. When I came to Toronto, there were no espresso cafes. I was here for two or three months and there was no place to have an espresso. I tried to find a job and sent out applications, but people said, "Help yourself." The government did not give you then what it gives you today. When you went into an office to hand in an application, people put you in the back. It wasn't because I was Italian. That was just the character of the government and the law at the time. It was very difficult to get a job. I generated an idea. I called my mother in Italy. She had a cafe and trattoria in Italy. I wanted to know what kind of coffee machine she used to make espresso because I had forgotten. She answered, "We have a San Marco machine. What do you want to do, open a cafe?" I wrote to the company in Italy and started to import the machine. I sold the machines from my garage.

Since people in Canada did not know what espresso or cappuccino was at the time, I approached Italian immigrants that were opening restaurants, social clubs and bakeries to sell my machines. It was a tough time, because very few people were interested or had the money to buy my machines. So, I decided to open my first cafe at St. Clair and Dufferin (called San Marco) to showcase the machine that made espresso and cappuccino. I also made authentic Italian gelato and pizza. The place became a success and also helped me sell more machines.

Was the focus on food or espresso?

MD: At that time, I focused more on food because Italian immigrants didn't really have a place to eat good Italian food. I also saw an opportunity to try and sell commercial espresso machines by inviting potential customers to the restaurant to try the food and see the espresso machine that I had imported from Italy so they could enjoy a good espresso, like back home. This was like showcasing the San Marco machine in a true Italian environment and explaining to customers that every good meal must end with a good espresso. The cafe/restaurant

was the start of a new opportunity for me. I was able to convince other restaurateurs and Italian bakeries in the neighborhood to order an espresso machine for their business. I would take an order and have the manufacturer ship the machine to Toronto. I would pick the machine up from the freight forwarder and deliver, install, and train the owner and staff to operate the machine in order to make the perfect espresso. It became my passion to provide the customer with the full service. I guess at the time, I was operating two businesses to see which one would best provide for my young family. I had just started out in a new country, with very little support from the government and banks. I truly enjoyed bringing some Italian culture to both the many Italian immigrants that lived in the neighborhood, as well as other nationalities that also immigrated to this new country to start a new life.

There was a sense of community.

MD: Yes. But I also wanted to provide my customers with a show by having the pizza maker throw the pizza dough in the air while Neapolitan music played in the background. I also imported a gelato machine from Italy and prepared my own homemade gelato. I then sold the restaurant on St. Clair and opened another one on the corner of Bay and Dundas. Here, I also started to offer pizza delivery within the downtown area. I guess the restaurant business was a good kick-start to promoting Italian culture to a new city and country. I was able to meet many people from different cultures and, of course, I had many Italians from Italy also coming to try my food and discuss business opportunities.

And from there did you go to Faema?

MD: One day the export manager from Faema Italy visited me at my restaurant at Bay and Dundas and noticed that I had a San Marco machine. He asked me where I had purchased the machine and I told him that I imported it directly from Italy and that I also sold machines to other businesses in the city, like restaurants and bakeries. He then asked me if I would be interested in selling Faema espresso machines instead of the San Marco brand. I saw this as a great opportunity as Faema was recognized as the world leader of espresso machines. From our meeting, I was able to sign an agreement with Faema Italy to become the exclusive importer and distributor for Canada.

When I started selling Faema machines and the business began to succeed, I put more focus on the business and opened my first showroom at Bloor and Lansdowne. Eventually, I moved to Davenport and Ossington where I established my routes. Shortly after, I also began to import other Italian equipment such as gelato machines, pasta machines, pizza ovens and complete, modular bar systems. Basically, all the equipment needed to set up a complete Italian cafe or restaurant. I believe that this strategy helped me succeed as I became known as a one-stop shop with the complete line of equipment and experience required to assist customers in opening a business here in Canada.

As my children became more involved with the business, they helped and encouraged me to open some retail stores in key locations to expand the business and further strengthen the Faema brand. Our approach has always been to represent the top brands in the industry, and we are proud to represent Faema, Jura, Moretti Forni, ISA, Zumex, Segafredo, Trucillo, and many others.

Today, our new headquarters is located at 672 Dupont Street, at the corner of Christie, the site of the former Ford factory where the famous Model T was built. The acquisition of this prize property was one of the most significant and meaningful events for me and my family. The building was completely restored to respect the history of the building and to house our new head office and showroom, as well as become the home of many other commercial tenants.

When did people outside of the Italian community begin to understand Italian coffee?

MD: As more restaurants were buying machines, the owners would encourage their patrons to try an espresso or cappuccino after their meal, and more and more people began to like the experience. I began to participate in trade shows where I would prepare samples of espresso and cappuccino for people to taste. My goal was to have people experience the true Italian culture of enjoying an espresso at any time of the day.

What are the characteristics of a good coffee?

MD: There is no secret; coffee needs to consist of quality coffee beans that are ground and brewed the proper way. A good espresso must have a good 'crema', or cream, and be full of aroma with a balanced taste. We usually refer to these qualities as the five m's of producing a perfect espresso: *miscela* (quality coffee beans), *macinadosatore* (assuring the proper grind of coffee), *macchina* (the machine must be at the correct temperature and pressure), *mano dell'operatore* (the barista must have the proper skills), and finally, *manutenzione* (making sure that the equipment is properly maintained).

People are more knowledgeable about good coffee and there are many chains like Starbucks and Tim Hortons; do you have to work harder because of this competition?

MD: I agree that people have become more knowledgeable about coffee and I give credit to the big chains that have marketed espresso and cappuccino in a big way to bring these products to the mainstream. As I mentioned, in the early days I was only able to sell my machines to the Italian and European immigrants. Naturally, because I sell and distribute espresso equipment, as the market grows, there are more opportunities for me as well. So, maybe I have to work harder to seize these new opportunities.

After this many years in Canada, what do you appreciate about this country and what do you miss about Italy?

MD: After the Second World War, there was this mentality of being self-made. When I came to Canada, it was difficult. I learned to develop my own business. I had some problems with city approval. I have been very respectable. If you want to stay in business, you need to pay tax and pay your credit, if you buy things on credit. For me, Canada is better than any other country. I go to Italy four times a year, so I don't really miss Italy. I am still an Italian citizen.

What do you hope is the future of Faema?

MD: I have four boys that have always helped me part-time during school, then joined the business after graduating from university. They all have their respective roles within the company and have helped me grow the company from a one-man show to an organization with seven locations with over 140 dedicated employees, as well as helping to secure the exclusive Canadian rights for several important Italian and Swiss brands. It is obvious that my kids share my passion for the business and for Italian culture, and passing the reins on to them has been smooth and seamless. I have eight grandchildren and hope that some of them will also join the company. In fact, some of them are already working part-time in the business while attending high school and university, and I see that they already express the same passion for the business.

CAMARRA
2899 Dufferin St.

Present owner: Elisa Camarra Valentini;
previously Domenica, Livio and Elisa Camarra

Opened: 1958

Menu highlights: maccheroni chitarra di mare—an Abruzzo specialty, pizza.

Fact: Founded by Oreste and Domenica Camarra in 1933 in Abruzzo. Camarra's now has a line of prepared sauces, dressings, breads and biscotti called Sapori di Mamma—recipes handed down over four generations.

Photo: Emilia Valentini

TRATTORIA GIANCARLO

an interview with Eugenia Barato and Jason Barato

How did you both start cooking?

EB: I was a married woman who did not know how to cook. My mom was a great cook. There are a lot of recipes that I wish I could have asked her for. I would always ask people that I worked with for recipes. One day, I just thought I would learn how to cook. I spent three months in the restaurant that we had. The chef would never teach me anything, but I learned with my eyes. Then I would come home and test out what I saw the chef do. I also read a lot of cookbooks.

What about you, Jason?

JB: Well, it initially started at home. We would have brunches on Sunday morning and the whole family would come over. I started just fooling around in my mom's restaurant kitchen. It was trial and error. I was supposed to be a lawyer, but when I found out how many more years of schooling were required to become a criminal lawyer, I changed my mind. My folks were wondering what I was going to do, so I bought a motorcycle. My dad wasn't pleased. He wanted to know how much insurance for the motorcycle was and I said, "What's insurance?" They told me I had to get a job to pay for the insurance, so I started in their restaurant. Initially, I was a bus boy but I didn't really have the knack for that so my mom said she would give me a shot in the kitchen. Once I got over the tension of being in a kitchen, she said she thought she could see a career for me working in the kitchen. It's a fierce environment. It's very tense. Once I got into that, everything fell into place. My mom taught me everything, but then I also learned from my grandmothers.

Then you went to George Brown, right?

JB: Yes, I went to George Brown. I was one of the first people from the school to go to Italy to train. I trained at Ristorante San Domenico, which spits out many top chefs today. It's ridiculous. But I also worked in France, Portugal, and the States, in Washington. I worked with a lot of great chefs.

Your background is Portuguese. How did you begin cooking Italian food?

EB: It is not that different. Take the dish "pasta e fagioli." When I was a little girl, that's what we ate. We didn't call it pasta e fagioli. We called it by its Portuguese name, but that's what it was. We ate a lot of pasta and fish. It's basically all of the same food.

So how did you decide to focus on Italian food?

EB: Well, first we owned a cafe. My mom did most of the cooking there. I wasn't cooking there a lot. Then, when we sold the café, we opened a Portuguese restaurant. We had that restaurant for eight years. We sold a mix of food though. It was Portuguese, Spanish, French, and Italian. It was a beautiful concept. But then we changed to something else because we got tired. We used to have a French restaurant in Oakville as well.

I love what we do here. The other day Tony (Barato) came in and he said he felt like eating pasta so I said, "That's okay with me." I tossed the pasta, with some fresh olive oil, garlic, and fresh peperoncini and it was delicious. It's the simple things. You will never see me cooking a complicated meal. That's not me. I love flavour, quality, and good ingredients. That's all you need to make a beautiful meal.

Is that your philosophy too, Jason?

JB: Our philosophies are almost identical. The only thing different that I maybe bring to the table is technique. I learned that. She didn't. I also enjoy simple food. I can appreciate a complex dish.

So where does your inspiration come from?

JB: I like going to a good market downtown. That's where my brain starts clicking. When you go to Europe it's a little bit different because you have all of these beautiful ingredients. Bloor West Village has these great markets, beautifully organized. That's where my brain starts running. Food is on my mind all day long. Sometimes, I'll wake up at four a.m. and start scribbling ideas until seven a.m.

So since you've started cooking, how has the availability of products changed?

JB: Prosciutto.

EB: Mozzarella di bufala.

JB: We used to just serve mozzarella balls.

EB: In Bologna, I had the most amazing piadina and they taught me how to make it.

JB: Tomatoes, as well. In the old days, we never got San Marzano tomatoes.

EB: When I took over the kitchen, I was very lucky. We worked with a company called Brunello Imports that used to provide us with the most beautiful ingredients. There has been a lot of change.

Have you had an influence on suppliers?

JB: We make constant demands.

And are your demands met?

JB: For sure. Always. We don't have a problem with our suppliers understanding our expectations about quality. Just the other day, my mom sent back eight veal tenderloins because she didn't like them. They didn't even question us.

EB: Quality has to be number one. I went to New

York for a short trip a while ago. We went to a place I will never forget. It was called Fiamma. It was unbelievable. The prosciutto, the quality of pasta ... it was amazing. It was a meal to remember forever. You eat to enjoy. But it's New York. New Yorkers can get what they want. We don't have that same luxury. They told me the name of the pasta and I can't get it.

Why do you think Italian food is so popular?

JB: It's not off-putting. It doesn't conflict your senses. It doesn't push you too hard. For example, I

Once you learn how to properly do something, it stays that way. That's Italy's cooking philosophy. You make prosciutto one way and that's it. They understand what's good and leave it that way. The food, the people, and the environment are all connected in Italy. Food is a pretty important subject in Italy too. Those were all the conversations I had in Italy. In Italy, you also get good value for your money. It blows your mind.

The thing that always astounds me is the mortadella. The idea of mortadella in Italy doesn't exist here.

JB: There's an ingredient that can be improved on here. It's definitely not the same.

EB: I tried a cheese the other day that was so good, but I haven't been able to get my supplier to bring it here. You have a little piece of that with some bread and you don't need much more. That's it.

What do you think the future food landscape will look like in Toronto? Will Italian food still reign?

EB: Yes. If they stick to simplicity, yes. If they try to be too innovative, they will not. So many new Italian restaurants open up and they play around too much with the food. Those ones will not last. I respect food. You don't play around with it. Pizza is made in a certain way. There is no reason to change it.

JB: I'd like Italian food to be more like Italian food in Italy. I'd like to see this happen within ten years, but it might take more.

So how do we make that happen?

JB: I'd like to see us start making a lot of our own stuff here.

Like the Eataly concept?

JB: Yes. Absolutely. It's a very visionary concept.

love Indian food, but I can't eat it everyday. It's too much. But Indians can eat Italian everyday.

EB: If you have a plate of pasta or a bowl of risotto, you will always enjoy it. You eat that meal and you're happy. Portuguese food might be heavier. It also has stronger flavours. You can't go wrong with a great plate of pasta.

JB: Italy doesn't let innovation take over its underlying principles of quality and simplicity. Other cuisines do. If you go for pho, you're eating a powder soup. You could never go to a self-respecting restaurant in Italy and eat a powder soup.

EB: I can't see that happening, Jason. The climate is different, the land is different …

JB: It's the husbandry of the animals that's different here. We don't even milk buffaloes to make mozzarella di bufala. Whatever you import from Italy will blow whatever we even try to make here out of the water. I mean, there's a guy in Iowa who is making a very good prosciutto. It's not the same as the one in the boutique in Parma, but it's still very good. Everything just moves at a very slow pace. I was at an Italian friend's house the other day. His homemade wine and his prosciutto were fantastic. This tells me that people can figure it out.

EB: The thing is that a lot of the local products cost an arm and a leg. There is a company in Niagara that makes great porchetta and other products, but it is very expensive. The flavour is good. It is not the same as in Parma. But there is no way that I can afford it. It ruins my margins.

JB: The last thing we want is for the generation that birthed us to die off and for us not to have learned their techniques and recipes.

EB: There were the Porco brothers who used to sell sausage and other meats; they were fantastic.

JB: That's what I'm talking about. It's like there is this gap. The older generation have figured this out so why can't we? That's where I'm hoping we will go.

What's your ideal dish? The thing you could eat any day of the week?

EB: Pasta with olive oil. It's mezzanotte pasta. I can have it at anytime.

JB: Mine is the same. But my death meal is a béchamel lasagna.

EB: How can you eat that everyday? It's heavy.

JB: That's my death meal. I'm not saying it should be yours.

EB: I can have pasta two to three times a week without doing any harm to my body. Lasagna is totally different!

Which Italian ingredient has been the most important and has changed how you cook?

EB: Tomatoes. The quality has improved so much.

JB: I agree with that. But I would say olive oil. When we started cooking, the olive oil we used was almost like car oil. The olive oil we have now is much better than what we were using back then.

EB: We've always had good olive oil though. I can't remember not having good olive oil.

JB: The other thing is the pasta. That has really improved. When we made fresh pasta in the old days, we didn't have semolina or anything. We had to use all-purpose flour.

EB: Yes, that is true.

JB: I have to tell you, I was at an Italian place the other day. I was very surprised watching this woman cook penne. She cooked the penne. Then she dumped it into this short ribs sauce and then she cooked it for another 15 minutes. I thought that was crazy. It's weird. I can handle overcooked meat, but not pasta.
A lot of people will send pasta back because it's too raw. We'll take it back. I mean, we are part of the customer service business, so we will just cook it longer for them. It's amazing.

A lot of it is still educating people I'm sure.

JB: Yes. Now that I think about it, that's where I'd like Italian food culture to be in a decade. I'd like to have a more educated clientele. I feel like sometimes we are de-training ourselves to make our clientele happy.

EB: One time, someone here ordered carpaccio. It went to the table. The waitress came to me and said the customer wanted to know if I could cook the carpaccio. I said, "If you don't know what it is that's one thing, but don't insult me by asking me that. Carpaccio is raw." I got upset. A lot of people just don't know.

COMMISSO ITALIAN BAKERY
8 Kincort St., 33 Eddystone Ave.

Owners: Frank and Joe Commisso
Opened: 1957

Highlights: nineteen kinds of artisanal bread, tavola calda.

Part convenience store, bakery, and hot table. Commisso Bakery is open 24 hours a day, 7 days a week, 365 days a year. Fresh bread is baked every few hours. Tavola calda includes veal cutlets, porchetta, arancini, stuffed peppers, lasagna and more. A favourite late-night stop for truck drivers and club-goers, it has remained largely unchanged since it opened.

Photo: Deborah Verginella

GRANO

an interview with Roberto Martella

What makes Italian food almost universal in its appeal?

RM: For me, Italian food is more than just the act of nutrifying oneself. Some years ago there was an exhibit at the Guggenheim Museum called "The Metamorphosis of Italy." It traced Italy from postwar through the mid-1960s and the curator of the exhibit claimed that Italy is the world's greatest cultural exporter. And one of its biggest exports is the table. This is the most significant aspect of Italian food: it has followed the Italian immigrants to the four corners of the world. And it's echoed appreciatively by Piero Antinori, a great Italian winemaker and legendary figure in the world of wine, who created the first really great Tuscan wine. He talked about how the beauty of Italy, where wine and food are concerned, is that they can exist at the most basic level and are good, healthy, and tasty with integrity, to the loftiest levels with the king's court or the president's residence. Antinori said that it was thanks to the Italian immigrants that foodstuffs and wine followed them, and then these products distinguished themselves by their quality, and then they became international staples. The cultural aspect cannot be overstated. It gives definition to subsequent generations.

The Italians have a wonderful expression: "A tavola non s'invecchia mai"—one doesn't grow old at the table. The time spent at the table is obviously very important because it keeps us alive and it contributes to the gentle aging process but it's a valuable time because you rarely eat alone. We exchange news and business around the table. There isn't an event—happy or sad—that isn't marked by the sharing of food, affection, and information with each other.

If you open up the Yellow Pages, the overwhelming majority are Italian restaurants. It's the most popular, accessible food for different reasons: because it's celebratory, because it's the Mediterranean diet, because everyone dreams of travelling there, renting a villa or retiring there, because it's iconic. Italy's greatest challenge, regionalism, fractures the country, but it also contributes to its rich diversity at the table.

What was the food scene like in 1986 when Grano opened?

RM: I am Canadian born. My wife, Lucia, was born in Puglia. She came here when she was very young and she's the executive chef here. We were married in 1985 and before I opened Grano I did a number of different things. One of them was working for the CIBPA, the Canadian Italian Business and Professional Association. I was their manager from 1980 to 1982. Previous to that I had been living in Europe, touring with a Japanese drummer group, and then I was offered a job with this cultural impresario. My goal was to stay in Europe, to deepen my understanding of Italy, the culture, and the language, because after university, if you're sensitive about your place in the world as an Italian, you want to reconcile that. So I stayed in Europe for a couple of years, and then I came back and wanted to reconcile my experiences there with my life and culture here. Then I met a kindred spirit in my life, Lucia. She had studied anthropology in university so there was this synergy. So when we opened, this was a cultural exercise as much as it was a culinary and commercial one. It had to work on a commercial basis otherwise we wouldn't have survived. We had to prepare things that people wanted to eat. We can't just sit and talk about Marinetti and the Futurists and creating dishes that are abstract culturally. Italy had boomed 'dopoguerra.' It had become an incredible dynamic, modern place. But then one would come here to the conservative nonna and there was this disconnect. Italy was at once rediscovering its culinary traditions but creating new ones as well. That was the tableaux which informed what we were doing here: to create a place that operated from the business point of view but that also made some kind of cultural statement. We've been doing Italian language classes for twenty-two years—"Language and Linguine." That informs what we strive to do.

We were the first ones in the city to put olive oil on the table, which in Italy doesn't really happen yet. Sometimes you have to exaggerate and be a

little overzealous with the traditions. There's this mania now with oil and balsamic vinegar. In Italy, it's a regional-based tradition, and anywhere outside of Emilia-Romagna balsamic vinegar is rarely used. But we get people asking about aceto balsamico and we put it on the table. The wines that were available when we opened were very limited, but at the same time, Italy was undergoing a renaissance in wine-making. The wines were Veneto-, Piemonte- and Tuscan-centric, but now you get wines from all twenty regions in Italy. The moment in time when we opened was perhaps fortuitous because it happened at a time when there was an explosion of interest in Italy and in the Mediterranean, generally.

As the Italians say, "diritti e doveri" or "rights and responsibilities." So, if you want to say that yes, this is an Italian restaurant, with that comes certain responsibilities. It's not only about using Italian ingredients that are irreplaceable, like olive oil. The coffee that we're having is Italianate coffee because coffee beans are not grown in Italy. Italians take the beans, roast them to their specifications, perfect the technique, and create something that's Italian, but a number of the ingredients are not Italian. The water, whether it's in Rome or it's here, is always local water. I think that's one of the strengths of Italian food. It can be interpreted. It's "easy." What you see is what you taste. There's little intervention. Unlike some traditions where the sauce is everything, Italian tomato sauce uses very basic ingredients executed well. It's very harmonious.

How has importing changed over the years? Did you have an impact on it?

RM: Mozzarella di bufala is a case in point. When you start asking for something, you get it. Importers will say, "If there's a market for that, we'll bring it in." Wine is another classic example. There was a limited selection, but as young people with southern Italian backgrounds came in asking about wines from Calabria, from Campania, from Abruzzo, etc., importers started to experiment. Young importers today are the ones who are bringing in these wines. Restaurants are requesting them and the importers are taking the initiative to introduce them to restaurants. There's this symbiotic relationship. If we look at the scene at the turn of the century in New York, Italian immigrants were feeding products to people, and there was a lot of indigenous production of these products. Italian immigration really influenced the level of production here. A lot of Italian restaurants were responsible for popularizing a lot of products. You can find prosciutto plants here. There's one in particular in Niagara: the Pingue family is making prosciutto which is exceptional.

You've mentioned this cultural synergy with your wife— what sparked the desire for promoting Italian culture?

RM: It was always there. The act of studying and

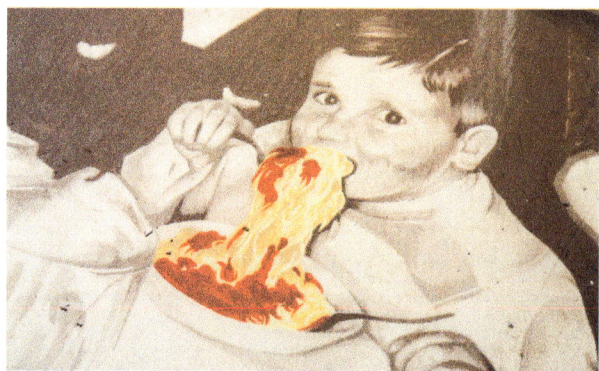

reading and reflecting about one's place in the world is important. For me, language is extremely important. I speak French quite well. The former Prime Minister of Canada, Pierre Trudeau, was actually named Pierre Elliot Trudeau. And I wondered, "What is the Elliot?" And it turns out, Elliot was his mother's maiden name. His mother was Grace Elliot. She was an Anglophone. That kind of fusion can exist and he had the duality in him and he nurtured that. He was a brilliant orator in French and English. He had the most brilliant mind in the history of our country. I looked at my own name, Martella. Yes, born in Canada, but even though in a young country we pay lip service to diversity and multiculturalism, there's this unconscious act of trying to be Canadian, to worship at the throne of Queen Elizabeth. Again, it's about *diritti* and *doveri*. We are all equals and can influence and inform our societies. We need to keep the language alive because in keeping the language alive we are more in tune with the world. Franco Prevedello was a mentor and a dear friend, and we travelled to Italy together. I saw what he was doing and it was a very magical moment in time. We both came from strong families with strong traditions, but you also need to break out of those traditions and make your own statements or else you can be suffocated by them. This was a way of making a statement about who we were and where we came from, but also who we are, and who we will be. We also owe a great debt to Italy and its culinary traditions. From A to Z, you have a lexicon of riches with which to create a restaurant. It's not just about what comes to the table, but what comes through the speakers.

You said Italians today are very proud of their own culture and very protective of a certain tradition. How can Italians preserve their identities and embrace life in Canada?

RM: It's certainly an experiment and a work in progress. I think that sometimes we need to challenge ourselves to step outside the scriptures of our culinary traditions. The French have a beautiful expression, "bien dans sa peau" or "healthy and happy in your skin." Yes, I love the Italian culinary tradition and I want to deepen my appreciation for it and my knowledge of it, but I also want to look at the Japanese traditions. They place a strong emphasis on presentation. And you learn about all of the new cultures in Canada, such as the Indian tradition, which is one of the richest in the world. It's not about always creating fusion because sometimes fusion can become confusion, but you can still experience other traditions. You want to encourage the people who are expressing them to express them as authentically as possible with the best possible ingredients. The two aren't mutually exclusive. There are, unfortunately, some people who feel that we must have a Canadian identity and to me that's more wishful thinking. We are strong proponents of Ontario products and feature local wines,

prosciutto, lamb, and beef when we can. Having a respect for your own cultural traditions means that you are more apt to have a respect for the local ones as well. The two can mutually co-exist.

Why did you choose this location?

RM: Franco Prevedello had bought the original building where you first come in. We were going to do something together, but then Lucia and I thought we could do this on our own. Perhaps we were naïve. When you think of it, maybe it didn't make the most sense to locate halfway between Davisville and Eglinton, but it was just happenstance. This was a very sleepy area. It's changed a lot. In some ways, we've been responsible for making it a kind of restaurant row. Back then, there was a greasy spoon across the street and a wonderful international cinema which I had visited many times before we opened here. We live upstairs, which is another important aspect of our existence here. We had just married in '85 and we opened in '86 and we started having children. We raised four children upstairs. In some ways, we've made the community our own and have a positive relationship with the community. We let people use the space a lot for local fundraising initiatives.

You've talked about people travelling and being exposed to Italy in a more direct way. How does your mission of communicating and living Italian culture fit into this new model of accessibility and how will this mission evolve?

RM: Good question. The fellow who created Eataly, Oscar Farinetti, is a good friend. We've had him here for dinner and hosted a dinner with him. He's also the owner of the Fontanafredda winery in Piemonte. In fact, I organized a press luncheon with him at the AGO because Eataly is part of the Slow Food movement. Only in Italy could you have the Slow Food movement start, in Piemonte in particular, which has arguably the richest culinary tradition in Italy.

Oscar created Eataly [the biggest one is found in Rome] to embrace Italian food. I spent two or three hours with him, giving him a tour. That could be something here. I used to have a company that imported some things called Italidea and that's very much a concept I could see doing well. It's about food the people can eat, food that people can serve, and food that people can take home. Seminars and courses are very important, as well as creating a centre with all of these things. I could see that sort of thing happening here because Toronto has become an increasingly international and cultural city. As long as all of the traditions don't all fold into one another, the culture is very rich here. People still want tactile things. They can watch a movie on Apple TV, but they still want to go to the cinema. They can buy the most pristine recordings on CD or vinyl but they still want to go to the opera house or to the live concert. We want to be together and share what we do.

Are you hopeful about this happening when you look at the younger generation?

RM: I think so. I think that the older generation needs to make that happen more and more. We are a very healthy community. We have some billionaires. As an Italian community, we haven't really infiltrated or informed enough of what happens at the Canadian Opera Company and the Toronto Symphony Orchestra. We have a dear friend, Tony Galliano, the Chair of the Art Gallery of Ontario, who helped put together the Galleria Italia, but that's not enough. We need to give an Italian take. What is an Italian take? It's a piazza. We need to create a physical piazza, but also a virtual piazza where there's humanism, sharing, and respect. The table can really be an important aspect of that. That's what we try to do in bringing people together here. As more young Italians become educated, the tendency is to question who you are. Instead of buying a Californian wine, buy an Italian wine. Find out where it's from. Is it from my grandparents' home region? We are fortunate in having such a well-known culture. For our "Language and Linguine" classes we have a little cartoon from the New Yorker and in it two women are speaking to each other. One is speaking about her new boyfriend. She says, "Now, we're taking it to the Italian stage." It's a culture that lends itself well and it's easy to become immersed into it.

Do you have any special memories that have happened at Grano or with Italian culture that have touched you?

RM: There are many. On a personal level, having two children work in the business now is special. Growing up, they worked at the front of house or at the back of house and helped out more than I realized at the time. I had a dear friend hosting a wedding shower and she wanted to do something out of the ordinary. She asked if I could do a wine tasting with the ladies and I said, "Of course." I brought my youngest daughter with me, the child who is perhaps least interested in the restaurant, and I was amazed at how adept she was at setting up and participating. It's been twenty-seven years and the kids still live upstairs or are away studying, but they'll come back to the restaurant and I'll introduce them to customers. Sometimes, the customers will remark, "I remember you when you were this high." To me, I'm constantly moved by that. The tradition keeps going on, people continue to be influenced, and people continue to come back to the restaurant. Like life, like love, we are constantly renewing ourselves. It's how we inform that renewal that distinguishes us. In fifty years, I won't be here and we won't be able to have this conversation. But you will still be here, and you will be a beautiful grandmother, who can inform her children and her grandchildren. That's what this is all about.

ITALPASTA LIMITED

an interview with Joseph Vitale

Let's talk about Italpasta's beginnings.

JV: I was a very young man. My dream was always to be in sales. My father's dream for me when we came to Canada was to learn a trade. We had different dreams. I was studying at a seminary for five years before I came here. My father came in 1951 and two years later, we arrived. My first job was cleaning floors in a chair factory where my father worked. It was located at Dufferin and Castlefield. In those days, that area was all farmland. It was very cold and we lived on the Danforth. I remember having to take the streetcar and then walk from Dufferin and Eglinton to this factory. All I had was the coat I brought with me from Italy. Imagine, I had just left studying at the seminary, arrived in Canada on a Thursday, and then the following Monday, I went to work with my father. On my third day, my father had to work overtime so I took the streetcar home by myself. I fell asleep and slept through my stop. It was horrifying. I was lost and I was asking for help but no one could understand me since I only spoke Italian. So I ended up writing the name of the street in the snow and eventually got home. My first week I made $24.00—$0.60 an hour and worked 40 hours. They took $1.00 in tax. I gave $20.00 to my father and kept $3.00 for myself. So I took my brothers, sisters, and little cousins to a variety store and bought them chewing gum. I was fifteen years old. But this is not what you wanted to know ...

It's perfect! Don't worry...

JV: As I was saying, I was always ambitious and wanted to be a salesman. When we immigrated I worked at various odd jobs until I found my calling in the grocery business. Did you know that the CHIN building that we're in right now used to be a big grocery store called Power? I worked in that store. They had a bunch of stores all around the city and then they sold them to Loblaw's. The store at College and Grace was one of the biggest grocery stores for Italians and Italian food. The manager, Gianni, used to play the saxophone in the store.

After several sales jobs in the food sector, I began my career at Primo Foods Ltd and worked there for over twenty-five years—helping build it into a strong food manufacturer. I worked my way up in that company to eventually becoming a shareholder. In the mid-80s, Primo Foods was sold to foreign interests. That's when I started Italpasta. We've come a long way from the two used pasta machines that I bought in 1989 to start the company. Now we have eight machines and are able to produce 170 million pounds of pasta a year. We have become the largest Canadian manufacturer of pasta—something I only dreamed of twenty-five years ago.

So you manufacture pasta locally and also import some pasta?

JV: Yes—we manufacture our pasta in Brampton and we also import a few Italian pasta brands to complete our pasta offering.

What led you to start producing local pasta?

JV: Well, it was really the moment when Primo Foods was sold. That allowed me to really think about what the industry needed—a "Canadian" manufacturer of dry pasta since all the pasta manufacturers in Canada were owned or operated by foreign interests. And we continue to produce in Canada because we have the best wheat and semolina right here in Canada. Manufacturers from all over the world buy semolina from Canada. We invested early on in the proper machinery and everything. We are located here, so why not produce here?

How important is this local production of pasta for our economy?

JV: Well, it's very important. It creates a lot of jobs for Canadians. Manufacturing is a big part of our local economy and people should be interested in buying locally-produced, Canadian products because this is what makes this country grow. If only imported pasta from Italy was available to purchase, how many jobs would that create in Canada? So, beyond helping the Canadian economy in this way, we also support the communities in which we

work. Import brands do not necessarily do that. I am proud to say that Italpasta is very active with charitable donations. We've donated to St. Michael's Hospital, Sick Children's Hospital, Crohn's and Colitis Foundation, G.I.F.T, Juvenile Diabetes, the Caritas Foundation, the Opera Company, as well as our recent multi-year commitment to Villa Charities—Villa Colombo Vaughan to name just a few.

Who did you target when you started the company?

JV: Italians—both as consumers and as a model for creating the best pasta. When I started my business, pasta was eaten primarily by Italians in Canada, so that's where I concentrated all of my advertising and marketing efforts. Italy is famous for making excellent pasta, so I studied how they do it and brought some of those lessons to Italpasta when I started the company.

What year was that?

JV: 1989. I thought if I made a Canadian product that was widely accepted by Italians, slowly it would come to be accepted by the masses. Everybody told me that I was out of my mind. They said that I would blow whatever money I earned. Of course, now they all say that they knew I was going to be successful and that they all advised me to go into the pasta business!

How can Italpasta compete with all the other companies that import products made in Italy? What is your strategy?

JV: Never stop working and never stop trying to learn and improve. Our goal has always been to create an excellent pasta. Thankfully, after twenty-five years, we have a very loyal following. We are the number one pasta manufacturer in Ontario and number two across Canada. You don't get there by offering a poor quality product. But we still have to

work very hard to convince people that locally made pasta is equal, if not better quality. Those who have tried Italpasta recognize the difference in quality. People often say to me that they can't believe that we can produce a pasta that is this good and made in Canada.

From a manufacturing and importing perspective how do you see Italian food evolving in Toronto?

JV: Based on the way immigration is changing, food in this city will have a more Asian or Indian flare. But that doesn't mean that Italian cuisine isn't still very popular. We recently had an interest-

ing discussion with a marketing firm that had done some research and, surprisingly, Western Canada loves the idea of la dolce vita. I think it's going to take a long time for that shine to come off the 'Italian culture' apple, specifically for anyone who is not Italian. For instance, if an Italian family goes out to eat, they may not eat at an Italian restaurant because they figure they can make it better at home. So they might try to experiment a little with different cuisines, but overall, I think it will take a lot to lessen the popularity of Italian food.

I've watched your commercials: they embody a nostalgia for Italy but also the idea of building a strong Canadian identity.

JV: Well, that's because Italpasta was started with Italian passion and built on Canadian traditions. Canadians are proud to be Canadian. I am proud to be Canadian. Even among other Italian-Canadians, the sense of pride for Canada is strong as well—we cheer for both Canada and Italy in soccer matches! Ten or fifteen years ago, there was a strong emphasis on buying American products. For our economy to maintain its strength, we need to emphasize buying Canadian. Italpasta is a Canadian company—our pasta is made with the best possible Canadian wheat, by Canadians, for Canadians. I want people to recognize that Italpasta's roots are Italian, but we have grown up a Canadian company. In fact, in the early 90s, Italpasta was one of the most vocal companies to lobby the Canadian government to stop the subsidization of Italian pasta in Canada. Not only were Canadian companies competing against Italian companies at that time, but also the Italian government. I am happy to say that we had a small victory for Canada at that time.

Do you define yourself as Italian or Canadian?

JV: I feel very strongly Italian when I'm in Canada, and I feel very strongly Canadian when I'm in Italy. Even though I've spent decades here, people still identify me as Italian. When I go to Italy, people look at me and say that I'm not the Italian that I used to be. So you feel uncomfortable. You don't feel fully Italian there or fully Canadian here. This would be difficult to understand for someone who isn't an immigrant to Canada.

Which qualities have enabled Italians to be such a creative power in Canada?

JV: Well, Italians are hardworking people. Maybe the younger generations think they can make something from nothing, but it's ultimately hard work that gets you places. Yes, I believe luck can play a part sometimes, but I believe more that the harder you work, the luckier you get. When I started Italpasta, people said I was a fool. Where does luck come in? Sometimes you have to make your own luck. You work hard, you get lucky.

You seem to see a big difference between generations. What do you see that is promising in the next generation of Italian Canadians?

JV: That the next generation is getting a university education. An education is very important. As a parent, I go out of my way to make sure that my kids get an excellent education. Although, this is true in Italy as well. But, by education, I don't mean that you have to be a doctor or a lawyer. I mean you have to gain knowledge. Knowledge is power.

What makes your products distinct from others?

JV: What makes Italpasta different? Definitely our thick wall technology. If you look at penne from the side, the thickness of the shape is called the wall. Our wall is one of the thickest of any pasta on the market. This is a gift for a busy mom at mealtime. If she is distracted by her kids and accidentally overcooks the pasta, it won't ruin dinner, but if she did the same thing with a pasta that has a thinner wall, dinner would be mush. We started using this technology first for our Food Service business because they have a pre-cook and hold pattern. We then applied it to our retail pasta. It's been a part of our success. It's made our pasta foolproof—and it makes for great leftovers.

So you've adapted your pasta to a North American lifestyle?

JV: I don't think we've adapted it. We simply created Italpasta based on how Italians manufacture pasta. Now, how Canadians eat pasta is definitely different than how Italians eat it. All the different types of pasta—whole grain, gluten free, ancient grains—now that's something you see more in North America. We do produce all of these types of pasta to meet the needs of every Canadian lifestyle. So, in that sense, yes I guess we have adapted our pasta—but you never lose the great taste you expect from Italpasta.

What is next on your 'to do' list?

JV: A lot of import brands want to partner with us. We currently represent Colussi Group in Canada—that includes the brands Agnesi Pasta, Misura biscuits, Colussi biscuits and Sapori Tuscan specialities. We were also recently awarded representation of the brand Bauli—known for their panettone here in Canada, and have just formalized an agreement with a dynamic, new, extra-virgin olive oil company called Costa d'Oro, from Umbria.

Italpasta is known for pasta in the eyes of the consumer. But, for example, we do have olive oil under the Italpasta name as well. Some people may think, "Italpasta doesn't make this oil, so why should I buy it?" That's where these import partnerships play a role. We are able to offer both the manufacturer's brand of grocery items, as well as our own brand to the consumer.

Was there a moment when you knew that all of your hard work was worth it?

JV: Every day. Just the fact that I can get up, enjoy my family and go to the office is good enough for me. I did what I set out to do, despite people telling me that I was not cut out for this business and that I didn't know what I was doing. I was able to succeed.

What has been your greatest contribution to the Italian-Canadian community and to the larger community as a company and as an individual?

JV: My greatest contribution to the community has been providing work for over 200 people for the past twenty-five years. I am proud of the fact that I still have people working for me that have worked at Italpasta since we opened in 1989. I used to tell the people on my management team that they are good at what they do and I would understand if they wanted to look for other jobs. Their connection to the company is not the same as mine—I've invested money in this company. For them, it could just be a job. But they still chose to work here. We are like a family.

Is there authentic Italian food in this city? Or is Italian food re-interpreted so that chefs can make use of local products?

JV: When I came to Canada, the 'authentic' Italian dish was spaghetti and meatballs. There used to be a place called The Spaghetti House at Dundas and Yonge. For $0.99 it was 'all you can eat.' It's not there anymore. I remember early in my career as a pasta salesman, I used to eat at this restaurant. I went downstairs because I wanted to see which pasta they were using. The Asian chef was in the basement and he was testing the pasta by throwing it against the wall. I asked him why he was doing that, and he said the only way he could tell if the pasta was cooked was if it stuck to the wall. Not exactly authentically Italian but again, that's not what you wanted to know…

I think authentic Italian food today is food that is simply prepared using fresh, seasonal ingredients. Italian cuisine is very regional and seasonal. We've taken all the flair of Italian cooking and given it a bit of a Canadian feel by using ingredients that are found locally.

Do you have a favourite Italian dish or Italian restaurant?

JV: My favourite Italian dish is Italpasta spaghetti or penne with butter and parmigiano. A very simple meal. As for restaurants, there are too many to name just one, but I do have to say I really enjoy eating at Casa Vitale—my wife Daniela is a great cook!

CONTINENTAL NOODLES
1664 Jane St., 602 Marlee Ave., Toronto
830 Rowntree Dairy Road, Woodbridge

Owners: Originally Franco Liberatore;
Present owners: Vince and Angela Liberatore

Opened: 1975

Highlights: St. Valentine's Day Pasta: red heart-shaped stuffed pasta for the lovers, and black heart-shaped pasta for the jaded and broken-hearted

Fact: Handmade pasta using traditional methods; supplies pasta to Scaramouche, Pusateri's and Whole Foods. Sarah, Vince and Angela's daughter, produces STLTO, a wine from Abruzzo available at the LCBO.

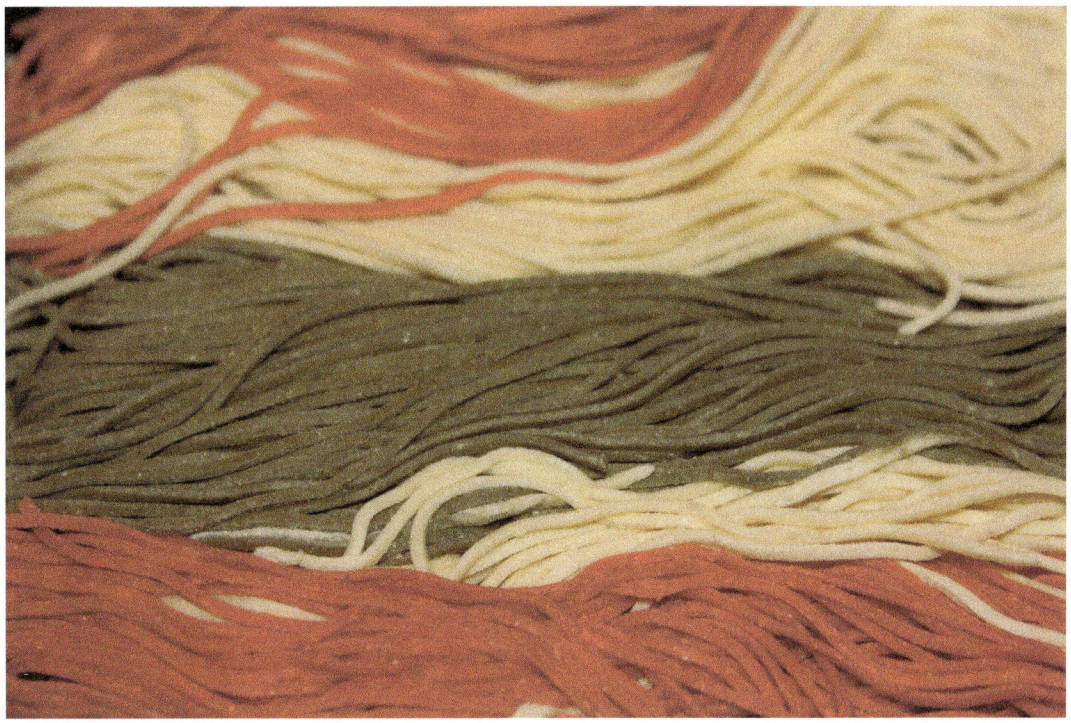

Photo: Deborah Verginella

LA FENICE

an interview with Rocco Fosco

Tell me the origins of La Fenice.

RF: La Fenice was started by my father-in-law, Luigi Orgera, a very well-known restaurateur in Toronto. He started Latina Restaurant in 1961 on the Queensway. It was very successful. Then he moved to La Cantinetta at Queen and John, and then he opened La Fenice in 1984. We haven't changed one single item from the menu out of respect for him. He passed away in 2000 and the family is still involved in the business. His daughter, Rita, is my wife and she took over the operation. She's the one running the whole show. I'm the chef. I'm a chef by trade. That's the story of La Fenice. As for myself, I'm not a big part of La Fenice. My wife is and my mother-in-law, Sandra Orgera, is. She's eighty and, as pastry chef, is still making the same desserts she started making thirty years ago. She comes twice a week to the restaurant. People know her. All her desserts are made in-house.

Are they regionally specific desserts?

RF: No. For example, the tiramisu is found all over Italy, but all the other desserts are her creation. We do pizzelle and cantucci and all different kinds of biscotti. They are handmade and prepared during the day. We don't use butter because our customers are mostly Italian and they prefer olive oil. Our biscotti are made with olive oil.

Are you Italian?

RF: I'm from Abruzzo.

How long have you been the chef at La Fenice?

RF: We took over twelve years ago.

What has your experience been like as a chef in this city?

RF: I have evolved, but I started to work as a chef here in Toronto at La Scala, Monte Carlo Restaurants, Mount Pleasant Lunch, and La Cantinetta, which is where I met my father-in-law. That was in 1976. The food was always traditional. I don't know if we could have called it Italian food at the time.

It was maybe Italian-American already. Italian food went through stages where chefs wanted to become something other than Italian. At the time it was called *nouvelle cuisine*. It never worked with Italian people. They wanted everything done just the way they liked. In Toronto, everyone always wants the same thing: a few pasta dishes, chicken, tripe, shrimp, and calamari. This is what my father-in-law, Luigi, served. He was an advanced chef and way ahead of many other people. That's why his restaurants were all very successful. All of the communities in Toronto know him.

What distinguishes the cuisine at La Fenice?

RF: Extra-virgin olive oil. In 1994, it was an unknown fad in Toronto. My father-in-law started to bring in his own olive oil and news of this was published everywhere, including *The New York Times*. The fish was also something unique. He was serving whole, grilled fish with some olive oil and lemon, and it became an instant success. His pastas were fresh. We still make the fish and the pastas the exact same way today. Everything was very clean with olive oil, salt, and lemon. We prepare everything ourselves and nothing beforehand.

Which region was your father-in-law from?

RF: He was from Latina, between Naples and Rome, near Formia and Gaeta. Fish is our specialty. The grilled tiger shrimps are well-known. After all this time, there is not much we can add. Anyone who is not in Florida or dead still comes to La Fenice.

With so many Italian restaurants in the city how do you account for La Fenice's longevity?

RF: By being true to our beliefs. We still serve the same food. The olive oil has changed, but we still use the best we can. Our fish is delivered to us twice a day by City Fish. We just won't change what has been successful for decades. If it's not broken, we don't need to fix it. Our food is good. Our ingredients are the best available. We do mostly fish and pastas. All of the herbs we use are fresh.

Would you characterize the cuisine as southern Italian?

RF: Yes, it has nothing to do with Northern Italian food. I would say it's close to Southern Italian—olive oil, garlic, fresh herbs, tomatoes, and onions.

As a chef, have you seen the public develop an understanding of what makes food authentically Italian?

RF: Of course. Customers have travelled all over the world and they know what good food is. There is room to introduce many more things. For example, I am working with tripe, rabbit, and quail and people like and appreciate this. First of all, this is what people in Italy have been consuming for thousands of years. Second of all, people know more about what is healthy and what is not, and they know how to balance. If they have a plate of tripe today, they will wait to have another one for a few months. People that like tripe will come here for tripe. Even people who think they don't like tripe will try it and then love it. It's the same with fried sardines.

How does experimentation come into play for you as a chef?

RF: I definitely do experiment, but I don't experiment with ingredients. I'm not into molecular cuisine. That doesn't interest me. I don't want to play

with a piece of lobster or meat. I want to respect it as best I can. We serve our lobsters poached with a little bit of butter, or if you want to do it cold with lemon or with pasta, that's fine. I'm not going to chop it and make a mousse out of a lobster. I won't do that. I don't believe in presentation. I like it, but flavour is more important than how it looks. In a way, our philosophy is to respect and not manipulate food.

Is this what makes Italian food, in particular, appealing?

RF: Yes. Definitely. Some customers don't even want their pasta plated. They just want it in a big bowl in the middle of the table so they can help themselves. A lot of the fish is from the sea to the grill to the table. It is nothing more than that.

For Italians, conviviality is central to life, isn't it?

RF: When Italians go out, it is for two reasons: they celebrate, or they want to eat something they can't find at home. When people go out to eat something they can't make at home, that dish is what the night is about. They aren't necessarily going somewhere for the atmosphere. But then, of course, the entertainment and the social experience becomes important. You remember it. That's what makes the whole thing so beautiful. As I said before, the food is the main thing.

What were your beginnings in this industry?

RF: I started as a dishwasher in Toronto. I had too much energy as a young person. After three months I couldn't take it anymore, and I started to move around to many different stations.

Is that when you knew you wanted to do this?

RF: Back then many immigrants fell into things. I liked it. I did it for about twelve years. Then I moved into the dining room and became a very successful server. After that, I became the maître d'. I started interacting with many restaurateurs. Then I started working at many leading restaurants in Toronto like Il Posto, Sotto Sotto, and La Fenice as a server. Then, in 2000, my wife gave up her banking career after her father's death. With her experience in banking and my experience in the kitchen, we came here.

How much did your experience in the dining room contribute to your understanding as a chef?

RF: Tremendously. I understand restaurants. I understand when people order what they want. I

deliver exactly what they want. Every chef should work in the dining room for a few years. Being a server is a great experience. Cooking is great and it's very important, but serving is just as important.

Do you think being a good host is part of the Italian nature?

RF: Italians are good by nature. They like to welcome people and make a big fuss about it. Sometimes people don't like that, but Italians are exuberant. Being Italian, good-humoured, and knowing the food, helps to bring the Italian fantasy into the dining room. You have more confidence and can express yourself better as a chef and a server. Many times I wear my chef's jacket in the dining room and will talk to customers very freely about things they want to talk about. It's a great combination and a great experience.

Why was the restaurant named La Fenice?

RF: This is the entertainment district and we are near the theatres. La Fenice in Venice is maybe the next famous theatre after La Scala. In 1984, when we opened, the only things here were La Fenice and the theatres. That was it. It made a lot of sense. That's the reason for the name. It's not because we are from Venice.

Has the clientele you cultivated from the outset remained the same?

RF: Yes. They are the same people that come here. They are all around. After thirty years many still come to have the same dish. Even Bob Rae still comes after many, many, many years.

What is your signature dish?

RF: Well, La Fenice's signature dishes are the spaghettini with lobster and the grilled fish.

What about your signature dish as a chef?

RF: I don't want to put myself in front of La Fenice. It's family.

What is your personal favourite?

RF: It's the grilled fish. The spigola or sea bass alla griglia. It's with olive oil and lemon. That's it.

Has La Fenice been instrumental in sculpting the current food scene in Toronto?

RF: Yes, tremendously. We brought white truffles here in the 1980s. We brought fresh fish and vongole in the shells. My father-in-law was ahead of his time: this is still his menu after thirty years.

What is the most gratifying aspect of this business?

RF: It's the interaction with customers and the relationship with food. I love going to buy food. It's very satisfying. When customers ask for something special, that is also always satisfying. Being with food and respecting the food is what it's all about.

Was your father-in-law inspiring to you? Did he mentor you?

RF: In the cooking aspect, yes. He knew a lot of things that many people didn't know. He was very creative. All of the paintings in La Fenice are his artwork. I wouldn't call him a mentor. I am the leader of myself but I really appreciated whatever I saw him do. Eating at his house and enjoying his homemade meals was great. What he did made business sense, too.

Is there a future trend in Italian cuisine?

RF: There is no trend. Italians still eat the same things they've always eaten. Presentation and molecular cooking are not the way Italian food will go. The food we serve today will stay around for a very long time.

Do you visit Italy often?

RF: Not often, but we still go every five to six years. We know Rome better than Toronto. Now, we have instant communication with Italy. We have Google. Back in the day, if you didn't know something, you would call. Now, you can just Google it.

.GELATO SIMPLY ITALIAN
146 Cumberland St. and 2076 Yonge St.

Owner: Alessandro Buccianti

Opened: 2010

Highlight: 121 flavours in rotation, affogato al caffè.
Fact: .Gelato is shorthand for punto gelato which translates as "spot," so, "gelato spot."
Signature flavours that have created a quasi-cult following include Lime-Cilantro, Spicy Mango, or Copacabana (evocative of the Brazilian churrasqueira flavours of caramelized pineapple and cinnamon), Reggiano e pera.

Quote: "In front of the ice cream display, we are all children."

Photos: Deborah Verginella & .Gelato

LETTIERI AND HERO CERTIFIED BURGERS

an interview with John Lettieri

Tell me about yourself and your background.

JL: I'm Canadian-born, Italian-raised, and Swiss-trained. Historically, our family was in the cheese business and we travelled a lot as kids throughout all of Europe. From the ages of eight, to thirteen or fourteen, our summer trips consisted of visiting cheese factories. We started in Holland and went down to France and the southern part of Italy. There was a big interest in my family in travelling and in food, especially cheese. After one year at York University, I did a stint abroad in Switzerland where I enrolled in a polytechnic that specialized in dairy technology. I came back fluent in French and Italian and I also became a certified cheese maker. I worked for two years in the family cheese business and at one point I started to go on my own. I started Lettieri Espresso Bar Café, a classic 'autogrill' kind of a place with espresso, fresh juices, cappuccino, and panini. The first location was 600 square feet.

Yorkville was your first location?

JL: Yes, Yorkville was our first one. That was in 1991. Lettieri started in 1986 as a deli. Then in 1991 we moved down to the city and created the espresso bar. We stayed with the espresso bar concept for about twenty locations. After that, we decided to slow down on the espresso bars and go into the hamburger business. Back in 2003, I thought there was a need for a quality hamburger that had real cheese and beef that had no additives or hormones. We signed a deal with nineteen branches out of Alberta that raise beef exclusively for us. We were able to source a product that was unique and exclusive to Hero Burgers, and we started the franchise.

How did you go from cheese to coffee to hamburgers?

JL: My dad sold the cheese business. When my dad sold the cheese business, we were unemployed. Then we entered into the coffee business. In doing that we began to understand retail in the small square foot format. At first, it was primarily a deli. I had an old espresso machine. This was long before Tim Hortons or Starbucks or Second Cup had espresso machines in their stores. Everybody was lining up for cappuccinos and lattes. In 1994

I went to the coffee fest in Seattle. I discovered Starbucks and I sat down in a Starbucks for a couple of hours and I began to understand that it was a serious business. They had about twenty stores at that point. People were speaking Italian: 'grande,' 'macchiato,' 'venti,' etc. When I came back, I turned the deli at Hazelton Lanes into an espresso bar. I got a new espresso machine and called the people at Illy Caffè here and they taught me how to make a great espresso. It just evolved. We had panini and tramezzini. It started off as a deli and it evolved into an espresso bar.

What is it that distinguishes you from a big chain like Starbucks or Tim Hortons?

JL: For the past ten years we've concentrated on developing Hero Burgers. Our goal is to open one hundred stores as soon as possible. We'll be at fifty stores by May and hope to be at sixty-five by the end of the year. Lettieri has been idling for the past seven or eight years. Prior to that we were the only place to serve the big lattes and the cappuccinos. We had fresh juices and smoothies. We had the element of soups, salad, and Italian panini. When we were strong in our heyday, a lot of it was tied to the whole authentic Italian cafe feel. That was the really big difference.

What was your niche market?

JL: When we started, it was really new to the city. It wasn't targeted to any niche. We happened to be downtown in Yorkville so it was a product geared to anyone willing to pay $3.00 or $4.00 for a coffee or a latte. This was not common before. Back in the day, you paid $1.00 for a coffee and that was it. Then Starbucks came along and it really educated everybody. Now everyone will pay $3.00 for a coffee. They don't even think about it. So that really helped. Of course they were a big company and they were able to communicate their message a lot better, but we had our niche in the Yorkville area and the downtown towers.

Has Lettieri contributed to the diffusion of Italian culture in Toronto?

JL: I believe that by introducing an espresso bar to this city we introduced a lifestyle for people to experience. This is what happens on every corner in Italy. It was dynamic and exciting and people wanted to learn more about it. As people started travelling, this experience was now available to them. There were a lot of espresso bars that were just doing espresso. They had espresso in the front and billiards in the back. I'm talking in areas such as College Street, St. Clair Avenue, or the Danforth. That was certainly available, so it resonated quite a bit with our clientele.

Did you grow up in any of those areas?

JL: No, we grew up in Etobicoke but we were always in the Dufferin and Rogers area because that's where my grandmother lived. My mother was born here but her parents were of Italian descent. They were the early immigrants from 1905-1906. We spent a lot of time with them growing up and that's where we hung out. Eventually we moved to Woodbridge.

Where are your family's roots?

JL: My mom's family is from a small town outside of Pescara. My maternal grandfather was from a small town in Sabina, about an hour outside of Rome. My father was born in Cosenza, in Calabria.

How does the Italian experience you try to offer fit with the North American lifestyle?

JL: I think it fits well because there is always an element of difference in entertainment. You can go to the places that you always go to, or you can explore

and find something different. That's what is fantastic about Toronto. You can go to ethnic areas in the city and get experiences that are 'out of the box.' I think the espresso bar was available to the type of person looking for that experience. You don't need sixteen ounces to get a coffee fix. We really started a transformation of attitudes. Spending a lot of time with Dr. Illy made it very clear that when someone has a good experience with their coffee, they will walk the extra mile to get that experience. That worked very well in Yorkville. People gravitated big time.

Why was it important to bring this Italian experience to Toronto? Especially given that you are now in a non-Italian food sector selling hamburgers?

JL: It was really a combination of experiences I had growing up and travelling to Italy. I had worked there for a four-month period one summer and also saw what was happening on the west coast of Seattle.

Those worlds were very similar. People weren't out drinking beer, they were sipping coffee. This was something that had gone on for hundreds and hundreds of years in Italy and I thought bringing it here would be effective.

As for the burgers, it comes down to food and quality. When I looked at the market, I saw a great sandwich—a burger—but I did not see any quality. None of the big burger chains offered a good slice of cheese or a burger that was seasoned with only sea salt and pepper. It came from understanding food, understanding the marketplace, and then providing something that had a mass appeal similar to coffee. We found it challenging to grow once the Starbucks of the world came into the marketplace because they were a stronger company and we were small. But with the burgers, we're the first in the marketplace to deliver a real piece of cheese, fresh-cut fries, and an honest piece of meat. These attributes are not a joke. It was a fluky idea but it just took off.

One year we sponsored the Canadian National Angus Show and I met with the president. This was about one to two years into our project. We had two or three stores. I asked him, "Where is my rancher? Where is my cowboy? Where is my guy that is making a difference?" He introduced me to a gentleman by the name of Christoph Weder who runs a group of eighteen ranchers that have taken cattle outside of the commodity and introduced standards on sustainability, how the animals are treated, and how the animals are fed. There are no hormones added to the animal. They do DNA tests on the animals. We've found that having exclusive rights to this product makes a big difference in taste and on reducing the carbon footprint. We take all of the hamburger meat, but the specialty cuts go to Switzerland and to Italy. There is a great push there to have Canadian Angus beef on the plate.

Your aim is to offer a good experience and a good product at a fair price. How can you do that and survive in a market filled with big chains?

JL: Their approach is different. We can't compete with them as a global company, but on the street, side by side, that's a whole different story. Lettieri has been around for twenty-five years. Right now, we're rebranding the whole concept to become new and refreshing in the coffee business. We're going to keep it very niche. We do phenomenal business in the Yorkville area and we have three Starbucks around us. Even though it's coffee, the whole experience is different. It's the same with hamburgers. We're in food courts and on the street right next to McDonald's. It's never going to be the same thing, it's a whole different product and a whole different experience. In these two huge categories—coffee and hamburgers—we're really able to appeal to a certain niche.

Is this niche populated by people who have an interest in nutrition?

JL: I think they're people with a high disposable income. They're well-travelled and understand quality. They're well-read. They understand that quality costs a bit more and if you're delivering great service to them, they understand it and they seek it.

How authentically Italian would you say your business is?

JL: You try to bring a quality product interpreted for a North American market. For example, we sell enormous amounts of lattes at 9:00 at night. There are restaurants that will stick to the core idea that you do not drink lattes at night and won't serve them. We try to take the essence of what the bar does and accommodate the North American market. With our new concept, we're going to try to get a little more niche. We've planned that the new cafes won't be open past 7:00 p.m. or 8:00 p.m. We'll adhere to coffee hours.

How would you describe your relationship with Italy?

JL: I'm a proud Canadian. This country has given us a lot. It has given us great opportunities. When I go to Italy I see how the core culture has maintained authentic ingredients that are untouchable, but at the same time, Italians are very avant-garde. Because of their economy and culture, they always have to reinvent or diversify. Going to Italy is a study of what's new and what's going on. Do we see how it can be interpreted for North America? I think moving forward. There was a period in the past where we lost focus a little bit. Even if what we offer isn't totally authentic, it has a good foundation in quality and has been reinterpreted so that it appeals to people here.

What aspect of Italian culture appeals to you most?

JL: Diversification. There are so many differences between regions, between the north and the south. Not being politically in tune, you tend to absorb all of the quality. When you become too entrenched in that, it can be a really sensitive issue. It's a one-of-a-kind place that has been able to survive in many ways by keeping the core culture alive.

Will the next generation have a similar appreciation for Italy?

JL: I think it will be geared differently, but I don't think it's going anywhere. It will get stronger. We have quite a few friends in the United States that are third- or fourth-generation who want to learn more about their heritage. I think when it skips a generation or it dilutes, you see people wanting to know more and more. They go back to their country and even if they don't speak the language, they are inspired and proud of where their ancestors come from. The last generation born in Italy was maybe two generations ago. Even though they're proudly American, there is a seed of love for Italy and Italian culture. I think it will get stronger.

Photos: Deborah Verginella

GIO RANA'S REALLY REALLY NICE RESTAURANT

1220 Queen St. E.

Owner: Gio Rana

Opened: 1988

Fact: Affectionately known as "The Nose," Gio's first incarnation opened on a side street in the Beaches. There was a bylaw against commercial signage, so an oversized sculpture of the owner's own nose was erected outside the door instead. The original restaurant had no liquor licence or bathroom.

Photo: Deborah Verginella

LIBERTY ENTERTAINMENT GROUP

an interview with Nick Di Donato

What were your beginnings in the restaurant business?

ND: It started with my roots. I was born in a small town in Italy called San Nicola Baronia near Avellino. My father had the neighbourhood bar. Everybody would go by for an espresso, a pastry, and maybe a little bit of lunch. It was very small. It was on the main floor of their house. He ran that for many years. When he came to Canada he tried a variety of jobs, and then he opened up the restaurant, San Marco, on St. Clair. It was one of the first Italian restaurants in the city. This was back in 1963. As a kid, I grew up in the restaurant business, often without my parents. My parents would be at the restaurant and my brother and I would be at home, but on the weekends we would be at the restaurant helping out, prepping things, cleaning up in the back, and stuff like that. When I got older, I would go out and greet people when they came in, and make pizzas. I later left my father's restaurant to start working in different restaurants because I was in school. Most immigrants aspire to have their children rise to a different level and to be well-educated and work in the corporate world. That was one of the opportunities Canada provided us. Those were the aspirations my parents had for me. I did go to university and while I was there, I worked in the restaurant industry. For most people in the industry, it's a means to an end. They're paying for their acting career or their education. For me, it was a means to an end in that I could work weekends and nights.

What did you study?

ND: I went to the University of Toronto and I studied engineering. I worked as a construction co-ordinator for Imperial Oil after that. My parents' dreams came to fruition. Their son was an engineer working for the largest company in the world at the time. I had a very good position and was able to travel across the country. I worked at their head office, but I wasn't happy. I still had the passion to be in the hospitality industry. The 9-to-5 job wasn't my thing. I didn't enjoy just sitting at my desk all day. So I opened a restaurant on the side with my brother and got back into the hospitality industry.

When was that?

ND: 1986. It was a sports bar called P.M. Toronto. I stayed away from Italian restaurants because I didn't want to be pigeon-holed as an Italian opening up an Italian restaurant. When I opened that restaurant I had no intention of working like my dad did from 9:00 a.m. until 2:00 a.m. I wanted to open one restaurant and then open another and another: I wanted to form a corporation.

So this was a plan you had in place from the start.

ND: I knew I didn't want to be a restaurateur like my father. I wanted to take it to the next level. I wouldn't have left my job at Imperial Oil to open just one restaurant. I wanted to build something significant and different. Many restaurateurs are prisoners of their own environment. My father was, and I felt badly for him. They always feel they need to be in their own restaurant. He was there from morning to night. We hardly saw him. He didn't have much of a family life. Restaurants are open on holidays and Sundays so you lose that family environment. It's a great business, but there's a different way to do it. From sports bars we went into nightclubs. Another thing I learned from my education was that today your restaurant may be on top of the world, but the next day you may not be doing so well. Things change. Locations change. Demographics change. I wanted to develop a diverse portfolio. So we did sports bars, nightclubs, fine dining restaurants, and casual restaurants.

Did this variety allow you to stay competitive?

ND: The diverse portfolio gave me a broader scope in terms of opportunities. I focused on the business of the restaurant. Some people do this as a passion. I'm passionate about the business of a restaurant. It's about food quality, consistency, food costs, quality control, and things that are on a corporate level.

How did this evolution from sports bar to the Liberty Grand happen?

ND: For me, understanding the hospitality business is what's important. Then you bring people in who can execute that. You have to have the ability to determine who the great chefs are and then provide them with the autonomy to grow in your own organization. It begins with the business model and then bringing in the right people to execute it. When I opened my first nightclub, I wasn't a promoter or a bouncer or anything like that, but I brought in people from other clubs who understood and I learned from them. As long as I had a good grasp on the business level, I was fine. I invest in my team and believe in them. I was fortunate.

When I opened up P.M. Toronto I had a different experience, perhaps, than other restaurateurs. We were right next to Maple Leaf Gardens, next to the most iconic team in the city. At a very early stage we learned the value of celebrity, and we were endorsed by Doug Gilmour and Wendel Clark. That was important to maintaining our restaurants. We started the Rosewater [Supper Club], and that was tied in with the Toronto International Film Festival; that was very important to us. We work with the sports teams, the film festivals, art, and fashion. This accounts for the differentiation in our restaurants. I'm always looking at the bigger picture. In Toronto I've found that the writers seem to like the underdogs, not people like us. What resonates with them is a small restaurant with maybe thirty seats where the owner is the chef and he is a slave to his environment. If you're not there 24/7 you don't love your business. I'm not sure that's the right direction for our city. It's a great component because it's a great way to give people opportunity, but to not celebrate large restaurants that give people a different experience is not right. I'm bouncing back and forth

between Miami and Toronto and I've found that the culture is totally different. The culture there is about the great, world-recognized restaurants. It's an alpha city and the city acts like an alpha city. It embraces the big restaurants from around the world. You have restaurants there that are in London, New York, and Miami. If you think of CK in New York, it's also in Los Angeles and Las Vegas. Toronto doesn't embrace that kind of restaurant. Or at least the critics don't embrace those kinds of restaurants.

Are people here more focused on the food quality because of the so-called 'foodie' culture that exists?

ND: You may call it a 'foodie' culture. I'm a restaurateur and Toronto used to be about the restaurateur and the overall experience. I'm passionate about great food, but it's about more than just that. Maybe that's why we're becoming the sleepy hollow in Toronto. If you go to a thirty-seat restaurant, you go there to eat and then you go home. There's nothing else to do afterwards. The larger restaurants give you the opportunity to make a whole evening of it, a process of entertaining. It's about culture, food, design, and entertainment.

How does being Italian infuse what you are describing?

ND: As Italians, we're about the cultural experience. In Italy, the restaurants aren't about just one component. If you go to the piazza in Italy, the biggest and busiest restaurants in the world are there. And those are not necessarily the restaurants with the best food, but they grasp the importance of the overall experience. The reality is that I could never do a small restaurant with thirty seats. By the time

I've paid my employees, there's nothing left over. I don't think small restaurant owners always understand the business model. There has to be a return on investment. But again, my biggest issue is that restaurants should be about the bigger picture. I just wouldn't want to have a restaurant that doesn't incorporate entertainment or design.

The latest restaurants you have opened, Cibo and Ciao, are Italian. How come?

ND: I think I have the confidence to know that I'm not going to be pigeon-holed anymore. I needed to do something very different and to learn from different styles of restaurants. Now I'm able to go back into my comfort zone which is Italian food. It provides me with another advantage and the experience of understanding fine dining and entertainment. I can bring that to the Italian restaurant. My restaurants are not 'mom-and-pop' or trattoria-type restaurants. We're large restaurants with good food and a great environment. The music we play is Italian and it's programmed very specifically for different times of the day. We're going back to our roots. It's real Italian. In Toronto people understand what proper Italian is and people from Italy can come here and say that we have authentic Italian food here. In Miami, it's different. The United States is more of a melting pot and they don't really have that. Their Italian food is really American-Italian food and they are proud of it. Some of the best chefs there will talk about New York-Italian food or South Philly-Italian food. They recognize that it's not really Italian. We've gone to Miami and we've gone with a proper, authentic Italian menu. We're not doing spaghetti and meatballs. Having the experience of multiple restaurants has allowed me to expand the idea of a traditional Italian restaurant.

What is the appeal of Italian cuisine for you?

ND: It's my comfort zone. I can eat it every night

of the week. I could never do that with any other food. In my travels all over the world, Italian food is the most prolific. I was in Zurich last week and the majority of the restaurants were Italian. It's interesting how a small country like Italy has a cuisine that can resonate worldwide.

Do we have a better understanding of what authentic Italian food is in this city?

ND: Obviously, the products and machinery that you need are readily available. I'm opening Cibo on King Street and the pasta-making machine and the other tools we need are all coming from Italy. We can source everything from Italy. We have access to more than just one olive oil, for example. You can make your menu more authentic as a result. Globalization is really helping the restaurant industry maintain a level of authenticity. In Toronto the key is that we allow all cultures to flourish. We're accepting and we have a more sophisticated palate compared to other cities. For example, we have the best Indian food in North America in Toronto because we have a large Indian population. We embrace multiculturalism. I think that's what Toronto is well-known for. Where is the city going? It seems to be toward smaller restaurants. In the next wave, I think we might see more alpha restaurants emerging. Toronto went from being the fifth-largest city to the fourth-largest city. As time passes, we'll have more growth and we'll be able to attract large restaurants with a great global magnitude.

What part of this business brings you the most gratification?

ND: I've had the privilege of meeting a lot of great people, athletes, and celebrities, in person. That's been great. This industry has also provided me with the opportunity to travel. For me to understand this business, I have to travel. I've travelled to Japan, India, Italy, Greece, etc. Those countries inspire what I do. It's a huge benefit. It helps us produce the quality restaurants that we do. I've been able to take this business from a small 'mom-and-pop' business, which is what many people expected it to be, to a very large business. We have 1400 employees now. It's multinational. I've been able to bring in a lot of people under our umbrella and to support them and to give them an opportunity. When I was getting into this business, people thought that you were getting into restaurants because you weren't smart enough to do other things. Today, hospitality is a professional business. Our executive chefs earn a good living and, as a profession, it's a living where you're not working 24/7. We give people the opportunity to spend time with their families. We've taken this industry to the next level. That's what I set out to do when we first started.

How do you define hospitality?

ND: To me hospitality is about being welcoming. It's about how you make people feel when they come to your restaurant. It's about the quality of food, the ambiance, the music, the décor, the presentation of the food, and how you say 'hello' and 'goodbye' to your guests. We're in the hospitality business and that requires an all-encompassing approach where we control the complete environment. It's not solely about the food. We've won awards for our washrooms. Why have I put so much effort into our washrooms? Well, that's also part of the dining experience. They're clean and well-designed. That reflects on what we do as an organization overall.

Anything missing on your 'to do' list?

ND: What we would like to do is create a brand that will resonate in alpha cities. I want to create a

brand that will have enough significance so that I could build it in London, in New York, in Tokyo, and it will resonate. That's where I'd like to be one day.

How do you balance work and family?

ND: Nadia, my wife, is our Creative Director. She does all of our interior designs. She's very much involved. She started working with us for the Rosewater. That was in the '90s. She has done every other restaurant after that and all of the clubs. She works solely for us. She's my right-hand person. She creates the environment and the ambiance and that's what we're well-known for.

When I was a kid, I mentioned that I grew up a lot without my parents because of this industry. I didn't take it lightly. That was the biggest negative. When I chose to come into this industry, I had to figure out a balance. I've set up a system so that my restaurants can run without me being there. I have that autonomy. It's about being able to let go and trust these people to do that for you. Obviously there are control systems in place, but that frees me up to spend time with my kids. I don't need to be at my restaurant on Saturday nights, which are the busiest nights, and can go to my sons' hockey games. I schedule them in my calendar and I plan everything way in advance. Everything else goes around that. I rarely miss my kids' hockey games and they always expect me there. I don't think they've missed their dad being around. They're great men and they love seeing their dad. They still respect me. We have a great relationship. They're not in this industry right now.

Do you want them to be in the business?

ND: No, I want them to do what is best for them. One of my boys is in medical school. The other may go into law, but come back into the industry on the business level. You want your kids to do bigger things for themselves. If they end up in this industry, that's great, too.

LONGO'S

an interview with Anthony Longo

When did Longo's open?

AL: Longo's opened in Toronto in 1956 at Yonge and Castlefield. It was started by my father, Tom, and my uncles, John and Gus. It was about 1200 square feet, it was a tiny store. It was just a family-run store at that point. We also had a delivery service that would deliver people's groceries.

Where was your father born?

AL: He was born in Sicily. He came to Canada when he was sixteen years old. My dad started the business when he was twenty-two. He just wanted to make enough money to feed the family and to make sure he was offering great value and service to his customers. From there it just started to grow.

Did you sell strictly Italian products?

AL: Actually, no. Since we were in the middle of the city, we had a variety. It was mainly a fruit market originally. Five years later the store moved to Woodbine and Mortimer, and it expanded to include a butcher, different produce, and a variety of other products. It was mostly Anglo-Saxon at that time.

In 1967, they went out to Airport and Derry Road, as a lot of Italians were moving out of the city and into Malton, and that's where you can see the Italian influence on the products that we carried: we had rapini and bananas and dandelions. They were products that maybe the Anglo customers didn't quite understand, but we introduced them into the marketplace. The Italians took to it right away. It's interesting now because rapini is on so many menus across the city. About twenty or thirty years ago, not many people outside of Italians even knew what that was.

As Italian food has become entrenched in our culture, how has this influenced your business and what customers find on your shelves?

AL: It helps our business when people are introduced to great Italian products, whether they are imported from Italy or made here. Ricotta is a good example. It's used in many recipes now. It's used in recipes that aren't just Italian. It's very versatile. The same is true for all of the different types of mushrooms that are used in different parts of Italy.

Apart from this being a family business from the start, are there other traits in Longo's that you would characterize as Italian?

AL: Because we're Italian we have a bias towards Italian food, so our pasta and sauce sections are broader than maybe some of the other sections. Even though there might not be a large Italian community in a certain area, we still carry traditional Italian products and cheeses and deli meats.

But I think we also try to cater the products in each store to the community that each particular store serves. Those are the basic things. Our underlying cuisine is Italian because that's what we are, but we try to cater to the marketplace.

How much of your products are local?

AL: On the produce side, the spring, summer, and fall products have a strong local bias. Right now we have rhubarb and many different types of berries. Fruits like peaches and corn will start in a month. We try to use as many local products as possible. In this climate we can't grow strawberries in January, but when they are seasonal here, we will use them in our store. We also support local greenhouses that grow peppers and tomatoes.

What do you import from Italy?

AL: Our signature olive oils are all out of Italy with the exception of one that is from Spain. One is Tuscan, one is from Sicily, and we also have one from Umbria. The pasta is Italian, the colombe, the

different types of water, and hundreds of other products.

How do you source the products? Through importers or by going to Italy on scouting missions?

AL: We do both. We collaborate with importers for a lot of it. Gente and ItalPasta are examples of that. We work with a lot of different people, but our team also goes to Italy to the buying shows.

Would you describe your store as high-end?

AL: I would say we are a high-quality store with great service.

From your perspective in the food business, how has the understanding of food evolved in Toronto and the GTA?

AL: I think if you've lived here your whole life it is something you've grown up with. We have 128 different languages spoken in this city, or something like that. If you take the time to walk through the city, there are so many different restaurants and cuisines: African, Portuguese, Italian, Indian, and so on. If you're born here it's accepted as everyday. When friends come from other countries and they're here on business or for a conference, they'll always comment about how they can't believe the variety of restaurants. It's something they've never seen before. I think Torontonians are spoiled by the amount and range of restaurants. There are five-star restaurants and more casual grab-and-go restaurants.

This must make your work more interesting.

AL: Of course. What often happens is that a customer will try something at a restaurant or while travelling and will want to try it at home. They'll ask us for the different products or ingredients. They may or may not be available but we try to get them.

How many Longo's are there presently?

AL: We have twenty-five right now. We will be opening up our twenty-sixth location in two weeks. We have an online business as well.

With so many locations, what is the experience you want your clients to have?

AL: We want to cater to customers who are highly involved in food and really enjoy it. They would typically be more highly educated as far as understanding the differences in food quality. They enjoy a good meal and understand and enjoy the ritual aspect of food: conversing with family and friends, or celebrating around food. They give us lots of feedback on what works and what doesn't work. That has been great.

What is Longo's future?

AL: We want to open one or maybe two stores a year. We want to renovate our stores. We're not looking to be the biggest in this business, but we want to be the best. We want to make sure our employees are well-trained and offer the best service to the consumer. We have no grand plan to open 'x' number of stores in so many years. We're privately held and the family owns and operates it along with a great team.

What is the essence of Italian food?

AL: I think its simplicity and the fact that it's healthy for you. The Mediterranean diet is back in the news: it's a lifestyle and eating style that has been around for centuries and it's just good, simple, and healthy. You can eat too much of it sometimes but it's great.

Do you travel to Italy?

AL: I try to get there every few years. I was there in December with my mom and a few of my sisters. It was a lot of fun. Before that, in 2006. All twenty-three members of my family went. It was great.

Will the next generation of Longo's stay in the business, do you think?

AL: I think so. There were three brothers and they each have grandkids. On my dad's side there are thirteen grandkids. A couple of them work full-time and there are a few working part-time, plus a few who would like to join later. My uncles, Joe and Gus, have grandkids that are younger so they're not quite old enough to work yet. So the answer is that, yes, there will be some Italian influence. It's something that we enjoy.

Would you encourage young people to get into the food business?

AL: I would tell them the same thing I tell my kids: do it if you have a passion for this business. It's a lot of fun if you have passion for it. You can't be successful at anything if you aren't passionate about what you're doing. Do something that makes you happy.

Which Longo's product is your favourite?

AL: There are hundreds of them. That's a tough one. My favourite overall is the homemade ravioli my mom makes. We have a similar product at Longo's but it's not homemade. It's a great one. In terms of other products, there are so many great ones.

And your favourite thing to eat?

AL: Easily homemade ravioli with a plain basil sauce. Food is something personal. I mean, it's something you put into your body. At Longo's, we reflect a lot on that. People trust us with what they put in their own bodies and their childrens' bodies. The food business has been great to us. You really get to meet and interact with a lot of people and learn from them.

I live behind your location on Ponytrail where you have a section called "gastronomia." How do you merge the essence of homemade food with North American lifestyle exigencies?

AL: Partnering with the right people in the store who prepare the products is important. For instance, making sure the sauce will be made properly. We try to be as authentic as we can be, but it won't be close to the food from any particular country, whether it's Italy or India. You just have to accept that from the beginning. You have to know it will just be different.

Can Italian products produced here be authentic?

AL: I think they can get pretty close. With things like pasta, the difference would be the water that's used. We use the same semolina wheat. The brick count in tomatoes is different from Italy to Canada. Our sauces are great and they are made here, but our passata and tomatoes are imported from Italy. That speaks volumes, I think. There are great products produced here as well. We have a lot of specialty cheeses being made right here in Canada and they should be given the opportunity to compete with the rest of the world.

MAGNOTTA WINERY

an interview with Rossana Magnotta

How did your passion for wine begin?

RM: I came from Italy as a young girl in the 1950s. We were raised in a household that was very traditional. I was one of three girls. As I grew older, I became captivated by the traditions that we had, and wine-making was one of them. Perhaps you will be speaking to other women who have different perspectives but what I honed into was the making of wine. My mother made the preserves, my father made the wine, and since I was the eldest of three, I felt it was my responsibility to learn how to make it.

Your father made wine for the family but not as a business, right?

RM: No, it wasn't a business. This was very normal in Toronto back then. Grapes were coming into Toronto from California. You would go to the market, inspect the grapes, bring them home, and use the torchio to press them. My father was surrounded by girls and he felt he needed to teach us how to make wine. He was a great male role model and since I was interested he thought he should teach me how to make wine. I was the winemaker in my relationship since my husband didn't know how to make wine. I was a biochemist and microbiologist in the medical field, and the passion for making wine and experimenting with different processes really excited and intrigued me.

That's what you studied in university?

RM: Yes. My focus was medical. Whether you check a person's blood sugar level or the level of a grape product, the chemistry is exactly the same. I found many similarities between making wine as a little girl and moving through the medical field. Of course, I was young so I wasn't drinking wine at the table. I would have a glass of water and then my father would pour one drop of red wine into my cup and I would watch it disappear. I felt like I was drinking wine and was part of the family. As I grew up, obviously the wine-water ratio changed. But that wine and food culture was important to us as a family, and I remember on Sunday mornings, waking up to the smell of sugo for the pasta. That's what makes Italian culture so different from

the rest. We take the simple things in life to another level. I think that's what makes people gravitate towards Italian food and culture. Back in the 1950s when we came to Canada, we sort of cast those things aside. But it's wonderful to see that we've come full circle. Our cuisine is not complicated. We take wonderful things from the earth and create fantastic, simple recipes.

How did the winery start?

RM: It was accidental because my husband saw an opportunity in the wine-making industry. It wasn't a winery yet. It was the *mosto per fare il vino* [wine must]. I had just taken some time off from the medical field to raise my children, so I decided to give my husband a hand. He needed a more technical background. We had to open the laboratories and then figure out how we were going to test these products. It was really challenged by the Italian, Portuguese, and Spanish men in that market: they were surprised a woman could tell a man how to make wine. I decided to write a little book on winemaking called "The Festa Way." I translated it into their languages and gave it away for free with every purchase. It had such a great impact on our business and allowed us to grow exponentially.

Then people wanted the ready-made product. They didn't want to make it themselves anymore. In this country you cannot do that. It's contraband unless you are a bona fide, licensed winery. We bought Charal Winery and changed the name to Magnotta. We wanted to further the experience of the Italian culture within our Canadian business. We opened

Magnotta in 1990. There were trials and tribulations with the LCBO at the time. In Canada, it's very hard to get into the wine-making business. There are so many policies and a lot of bureaucratic red tape that inhibit growth. We thought we would open this winery, pass it on to our children, and that it would survive us for many generations. We ended up going head-to-head with our regulators because we wanted to be treated fairly. It ended up becoming a David and Goliath story, and we survived it. We are now the third largest winery in Ontario by volume of sales in litres. We just purchased Kittling Ridge Winery, so that number will skyrocket. We have six boutique stores that we've changed from Kittling Ridge to Magnotta so the company can double in size over the next couple of years. This growth is very exciting for us. When we started, we took a chance. I have over 150 employees and an impressive portfolio of over 200 products. We were able to bring some very interesting products to the table. We made a *passito*, for example. We brought in the technology from Italy and then applied it to the grapes we have here. Those are the things that we've transplanted from Italy.

You are using Italian technology on indigenous grapes but you still can't call them by their Italian names, so are you re-interpreting Italian wines?

RM: It's a very new-world type of twist. My strategy is to give a high profile to Ontario wines. I am an Ontario winery with an Italian background. In many different industries here, people are not necessarily trying to reinvent the wheel, they are lending their own personality to the products. We grow Cabernet Sauvignon and Chardonnay grapes here. They grow these same grapes in Italy but they are a little different here. We have a different climate but we can do some wonderful things with what we have here. So, yes, I am not making an Amarone with the exact combination of grapes they would use in Italy or in other places in Europe, but we use the same process.

Our job in Ontario is to tell the world that we're up-and-coming in terms of winemaking. We've won incredible awards in Europe—not just Magnotta, but other Ontario wineries as well. We created the first sparkling ice wine and are very proud of it. We sent it to Italy in 1997. We didn't know what category to put it in. They had ice wine but this was sparkling ice wine. Italy created a new category and we've been winning golds in that category since 1997. They love the product. The bottle is a beautiful cobalt blue, made in Italy. The box is Canadian and so is the product inside but the bottle is Italian. It's a story of harmony.

We've been doing that with art as well. We have such beautiful, original pieces. Many are Italian because of our connections with Italian artists. Instead of creating a logo we decided to use art and we now have over 400 pieces of art and sculpture

from all over the world. Sometimes you put a piece on the wall and realize this is perfect for the product you are creating. You are communicating that to the customer. There's a relationship between the art and the science of the wine. Some people differentiate between the different Cabernet Sauvignons by the art on the bottle.

The relationship between art and wine is interesting...

RM: Well, you can make wine simply by fermenting the grapes, but wine is not just that. It's scientific, but also an art. When I talk about my wine I talk about it coming alive: it's a living thing to me and it evolves. Today it tastes one way, and if I open it many years from now, it will taste differently. It breathes and blossoms like a flower. Even though I loved winemaking as a young girl, I thought studying the human body was what I was going to do for the rest of my life. I thought of wine as a hobby. I don't think I respected it as much as I do now because now I understand the evolution. I can touch my grapes and the vines and the soil. You get excited about the harvest. It's very emotional during the spring when I look at my vines and think about what I might have by August or September.

What are the challenges of owning a winery and growing grapes in the Canadian climate?

RM: What most people don't realize is that the Niagara peninsula has a wonderful microclimate. People in Italy know we're popular for our peaches, but where we grow our grapes has the wonderful moderation of the lake and the river, plus the escarpment, which protects them from the harsh weather. We have a balance. Also, we have very cold winters, unlike Italy, and that really helps our ice wine production. Ice wine is Canada's ambassador to the world. It is harvested in the dead of the winter. We have wonderful summer weather for certain wines but also great weather for ice wines.

Last year was a great year. We produced red wines with such great sugar levels because of the climate. We have to tell the world. We are winning awards left and right. We have won over 3500 awards and most of them are from Europe. We were curious to know how we measured up against some of the best in the world, so we took a chance and sent our wines to European competitions. Canadian wines as a whole have been doing very well. We have the best technology because we import it, but we also grow great products. Our job now is to show the world what Ontario can do, and what Canada can do in the world.

You talked about the challenge of being a woman in the wine-making field. What do you think was your strongest response to those who doubted you?

RM: It's not what you say. I just stood my ground and strategized about how I was going to get people to listen to me. I was always challenged to speak my mind because my parents were that way. My mother was a dressmaker, but she wasn't a traditional woman who stayed at home to watch her kids. She was the original breadwinner in the family. My father allowed me to speak my mind. I controlled my emotions and tried to show the men that I knew what I was talking about. Over time they learned that I was not only good at it, but that I could use my medical expertise to help them with the process. If there was an infection or mould in the product I could show them how to get that out by using chemicals. I managed to earn not only their trust, but their respect.

In Europe and the United States there are many women in the wine-making business. We are statistically behind in Canada. It wasn't much of a problem in the customer area, but it was in the banking and administrative area. Bankers look at men as the cornerstone of a business, so it took a while to show them that I knew what I was doing. I was lucky to have had a very supportive husband who knew my strengths. Unfortunately, Gabe passed away three years ago, but even before that, I was already there. It was respect and hard work. My staff respected me as a female wine maker and a businesswoman. I was lucky enough to be successful in balancing both a successful career and family life. I became successful later in life because I was patient. I knew I wanted to raise a family and take time out for my children. I wanted it all. I think that women who are patient can have it all. I'm at a time in my life where I have a successful business, grown-up children, and no regrets. I did everything I wanted to do with my children. The only regret I have is that my husband and

I worked so hard to build this business together.

How have Italian food, culture, and wine inspired you?

RM: The liquor control board used to sell wine in a paper bag. You didn't see the wine. Then they opened up their beautiful stores. When we started, we wanted people to taste our wines at our stores and we very quickly gravitated towards food. The liquor control board does this now, but back then they didn't. On the back of all of our wine labels we had food groups or styles that would go with that wine. It would help the regular consumer that didn't know a lot about wine or was too embarrassed to ask to figure it out. We gave them that direction. We gravitated a lot to Italian cuisine because I love to cook and bake.

Where do you think the wine market in Ontario is headed? How will wine consumption evolve?

RM: Ontarians have an opportunity that most people in the world don't have. If you go to Italy and buy wines in the vinoteca, the majority of the wines are Italian. You will not find an Ontarian wine on the shelf. If you go to Chile, 99% of the wines in the stores there are Chilean. If you travel to the United

States, most of the wines are American. But if you come to Ontario, the Ontarian portion of the wines on the shelf is small compared to those from the rest of the world. So Ontarians have an opportunity to taste wine from all over the world and are the most educated consumer group. This also makes it very challenging for Ontario wineries to be what an Italian winery is in Italy or a Chilean winery is in Chile. It becomes very difficult from a manufacturing point of view. From a consumer point of view, the evolution has been wonderful. We're a little bit handicapped as an Ontario winery in that respect. It's tough to compete with that. Italy is at the top. They've had a lot of support to make that happen. I'm trying to bring the profile of Ontario wineries up. I'm trying to promote them as a great alternative to these other wines and to show Italians in this province that the products created here in Ontario are worthy. Italians in Ontario need to be just as proud of Ontario businesses as Italians are of their businesses. We cannot live in the shadow of Italy. I think we're supposed to create our own individuality here. We are Canadian with Italian DNA, but we need to be supportive of our own industries.

What would you say is your husband's legacy?

RM: Gabe had a vision to create a winery and give it our family name, to be proud of it, and to pass it on to our children. He passed away from complications due to Lyme disease. Our name is on the business so it's quite clear what the legacy is. I want to continue to grow this company and keep it successful. That's why I purchased the other winery. I saw it as an opportunity to extend it and to make sure that it was going to be viable and strong. This is a very regulated business in Ontario and you can only grow by having special licenses. The winery we bought already had these special licenses and allowed us to open up all of these stores. My husband and I put so much into this. I felt this was the next step I had to make.

I'm also building this research venture: The G. Magnotta Foundation for Vector-Borne Diseases. That's what the next phase of my life is about. I said in the beginning that I started in the medical field, deviated into the wine business, and that through the trials and tribulations we had growing the winery, I had been forging so many relationships. I'm back where I feel the happiest. I don't know if it was by design, but I've come full circle. I started in medicine, I used my business as a way to give back to the community, and now I'm back in an area that feels like home. I don't know if too many people can say that. I lost the most precious part of my life, my husband, and now today, I need to make this happen for his life and for everybody else that is dealing with the same ailment. When I've accomplished that, I will say that I've been successful.

IL GATTO NERO
720 College St.

Owners: Carmine and Michael Raviele

Opened: 1960

Highlights: espresso, pizza da Michele, spinelli (folded pizza bread with different fillings), arancini.

Fact: A Little Italy institution. You can always catch the FIFA World Cup games or Formula One races here over Carmine's legendary espresso. Actor Paul Sorvino drank his while singing opera at the bar when he was in town shooting. At night, Michael extends his earthy welcome to a decidedly hip clientele. Known as the Black Cat by those in the neighbourhood, it remains the meeting place for the older Italians still here and the newer residents of Little Italy.

Photo: Denis De Klerck

FABBRICA

an interview with Mark McEwan

What is your first memory of food?

MME: My first memory of food? That's very simple. I come from a family of small-town farmers in Ontario and Scotland. Food was always a big deal on both sides of the family. Both of my grandmothers could whip up a meal for fifteen people in an hour and a half's notice. They had stock, fruit preserves, root cellars, and dried meringues for desert. They were both capable of putting food on the table at a snap of a finger. My mother was, and still is, an excellent cook, so it was very much part of the family. On the McEwan side, my grandparents had this root cellar and it was just amazing to me to see all of the root vegetables and preserves that were being held all winter long. They were living old school. So it was there from day one.

Is there a specific dish that you remember putting in your mouth and thinking "Wow!"?

MME: Yes. I'm going to say this and it might seem like I'm conjuring this up because it has sort of become street cool, but my grandmother Devlin used to own a Lucky Dollar Store on Mount Pleasant, which was the grocery store, the post office, the butcher shop, and all of those things. When she made mac and cheese, they would take a bone-in ham and this big wheel of white cheddar and make it. As a kid, I would die for it. As a visual, it's not exactly glamorous, but it was truly beautiful.

That's interesting. I think it was MFK Fisher who recalled a fried egg sandwich on wax paper as her earliest memory of something divine. It had to be on wax paper.

MME: It was perfect at the moment. That's where food has come to in Toronto. The sophisticated dining crowd in Toronto wants simple food, but done well. The done well part is the critical part.

Your career has gone from the Sutton Place Hotel to Pronto to a present which sees you presiding over Bymark, Fabbrica, One, and North 44, to name a few. At this point, where do your inspirations come from?

MME: I definitely trust my instincts. I look a lot at what other chefs are doing as well and try never

to copy, but you do draw influence from the way everyone interprets. We were just in the back kitchen talking about pastries. I was talking to Amy here at One and I said, "I want you to put a white cake on the menu, and I want you to call it "white cake." I want you to accompany it with the fruits of the season. The inside should be white, the icing should be white, and there should be a little bit of coconut involved, but that would be it." It will just be a white cake so supple that it will melt in your mouth. People go crazy for it.

Is that something inspired from your past?

MME: Yes. My mother, if I'm being honest, used to use boxed cake mix and make white cakes. My grandmother would make the most perfect white cakes with great icings and the fruits of the season. In the winter, you add preserves instead. We had a meeting today where we talked about putting a re-invented banana split on the menu here. I still love bananas. I remember eating banana popsicles as a kid and it was my favourite flavour of all of the popsicles. It still resonates with me. But when you do these things, you do them well.

In the early part of your career, you were very much French-influenced. When did Italian food become a part of your dictionary?

MME: When I bought Pronto from Franco [Prevedello]. It was very funny. Much of Franco's cooking at the time wasn't even really Italian. It was nouveau Italian and it would have driven the Italians crazy, but it was very successful. So initially my cooking was French and Italian there. I embarked on my journey with Italian food and I love it.

Did Italian food supplant French food for you?

MME: It definitely took the focus off. It was the water we were all swimming in. Toronto was a very young city in terms of food and I arrived just as it was transitioning from hotel to restaurant, from steakhouse to a modern interpretation of food. If you weren't Italian, Greek, or Spanish, you would never eat a whole fish back in the day. You didn't know about balsamic vinegar or San Marzano tomatoes, which have become staples in the kitchen today. The Italian community did. I understand why they used to snicker and laugh at us. We were trying, but we didn't get it. Today, I think we get it. In Woodbridge back in the 1970s, everyone had a cantina and they made their own tomato sauce and sausage. People used to laugh about them having these things and all of the sausages hanging from the wall. It was not something people admired, but today it has become cool. Chefs do those things. It took a long time for us to get it, but at least we got it.

What is it about Italian food that makes it universally loved?

MME: It's approachable. You can eat it four or five times a week in different forms. It's not a cuisine that overwhelms you. For instance, I find that I can only eat sushi once every ten days. I can't have a rich, fancy French meal on a regular basis. There are some Italian places that you can go to where you can eat from the menu seven days a week. It's simple, but it's not. It appears simple and it's wonderful and wholesome and tasty, but you have to nail it every single time.

What is your favourite dish or ingredient?

MME: It's hard to say. I love octopus. I could eat it in all forms every single day. We do it in a salad with chickpeas and salumi and arugula and a nice vinaigrette. But I love making terrific brodo and starting a braise on a pork shoulder. I love making soft polenta and fresh gnocchi and pasta. To say you like one better than another is really hard. That's the essence of Italian food: whether you are making a fennel salad with orange or a swordfish steak, it's all fabulous.

How has the availability of products changed since you started? And how have you influenced what the suppliers choose to import?

MME: In the early stages, supplies were meagre. The funny thing is that food is Italy's biggest export. Since it's Italy's biggest industry, today it's very easy to find products of various qualities on the market. I don't get as captivated with white truffles as I used to just because the cost of them is prohibitive, but I get excited about Caputo flour, good ricotta, and good buffalo mozzarella. If you come to my store and you look at the vinegar and oil shelf, it's about seventy feet long and it's just crammed with products that are the best in the world. Italy is the best in the world.

As a chef and restaurateur, how much have you influenced what suppliers bring in?

MME: On a personal level, we've always bought the highest quality products and have always supported the suppliers when they bring them in. I wouldn't say that I had a huge influence on a personal level, but I think that, together with a bunch of other chefs, we were the ones who were buying the products and we influenced the city with our menus. It's one big pond we swim in and it's interesting to see how it has evolved. I bought Pronto from Franco with two other gentlemen in 1985 so it has been a long road, almost thirty-three years now.

Is there a product that changed your cooking?

MME: I think San Marzano tomatoes and Italian olive oil are standard in all five of my loca-

tions. We don't buy anything but that. I would add Caputo flour to that list as well. Those are standard building blocks in my kitchen. We don't work with anything else. It never changes. You can bring in shiny, little objects as ingredients. That's easy to do. I love the fact that Italy pays so much attention to the simple stuff. There's no bastardization of the product, and if there is, there's going to be a fight.

Where is Italian food going in this city?

MME: I think the whole process of change is going to slow down because we've finally gotten it right. You're going to judge chefs based on technique. You will go to five different restaurants and have gnocchi with a fresh heirloom tomato sauce and then judge which is best. The change will come in the refinement of the technique and how dedicated the chef is in picking perfect ingredients, managing them well, and running a restaurant. That's where the competition should be. It's not about reinterpreting a basic product. It has merit, but that's not the game I'm chasing. I love the old school technique.

How have your clients developed? Have their expectations changed?

MME: We have really tough clients. They're great, but they're tough. There's no fooling them. They are well-travelled. I tend to deal in the high-end restaurant business so I see people who have travelled to more places than I have and more frequently. They've eaten in more three-star Michelin restaurants than I have in my career. They're a tough audience, so you have to work hard.

Which products do you import and what do you source locally?

MME: All of our produce is sourced locally. Our protein is generally sourced from within Canada.

Some of the fish is flown in from the west coast. A great deal of it. All of our basic ingredients such as San Marzano tomatoes, spices, flours, and different salts are all imported. We only buy the best of the best of the best. We try to be supportive of local growers, but the reality is that our seasons are very short. Blackberries were here, but because we had a very wet season, they were gone. You try to grab them when you can.

In the winter, do you rely on preserves that you've made or do you import?

MME: We do both. I can't be serving my clients onions, apples, turnips, and squash all winter. We shop the world for the best products and we do it thoughtfully. We buy sustainable fish 95% of the time. I feel guilty when I serve yellow fin because I know the state of the market isn't great. It's still on the menu so it's 100%. They're tough goals to achieve. The idea of farm-to-table is a bit overdone. Every chef says the same thing. I don't preach it or use it as a term, but I shop local whenever I can. I'm a big proponent of PEI beef. I represent their certified Angus program. I think it's one of the greatest Canadian food stories that exists. That island is so pristine. I don't know if you've spent much time there. We have thirty-seven farmers that raise cattle for slaughter. The only reason it works is because the government built a co-op abattoir. So there are all of these individual farmers who keep these well-kept farms that look like they're out of the 50s. Families are running them. They bring in fifteen to twenty heads to be slaughtered and then that goes to general market. The beef is naturally pasture-raised and finished on grain and potatoes. It's such a great story because this island is surrounded by ocean and it's such a perfect environment for these animals to be raised in. There are no chemicals of any sort or hormones. It's as natural as you can get in this market and no one ever talks about it. If it were in Europe we would be hailing it for the sea winds that fall on the grass, but because it's in PEI we don't talk about it. I promote it. I promote it more than I do Alberta, although I do still buy some Alberta beef. Their farms are huge.

Do you travel to Italy?

MME: Oh yes. I love it. We travel more to Italy than to any other country on the planet.

Your cooking isn't regional, but is there a specific or, perhaps, a newer region that has taken your fancy?

MME: I know how passionate Italians are about where they live. You can get in a bar brawl very quickly over it. I love southern and northern Italy. I like the conversation that never ends.

Is there anything Italian that you've discovered in the last little while that has impressed you? You're being very diplomatic.

MME: What wows me about Italian food is that less is more. As a chef, that's a very difficult concept to wrap your head around. There has definitely been an education. You really underestimate Italian food when you first look at it and as a young chef with a lot of moxie that can be a problem. As you get older you understand how important that subtlety is and how hard it is to obtain. That's what amazes me about Italian food.

So where does the chef part come in?

MME: I try to honour the products in a traditional way. My Italian cooking is not interpretative. It's just trying to do what has been done before. I like being told what to do for a change. I really like having a guidebook and a set of rules. Now, from a presentation point of view, I guess you can interpret things a little bit. If you look at Fabbrica as an example, we follow the rules on everything.

We do funny things like "Nonna McEwan's Ravioli," but everyone has to have a sense of humour. It's like me doing kosher food. We did a kosher division this year and the Jewish community has really embraced us. But we managed to get through the politics of all of that because we serve good food. It's amazing what serving good food can do! I have many old school Italians that come to Fabbrica and they love it.

INNISKILLIN WINES
Niagara-on-the-Lake

Co-founders: Donald Ziraldo and Karl Kaiser

Founded: 1974

Fact: Inniskillin was the first winery licence issued since prohibition in 1929. Ziraldo was the founding chairman of the VQA (Vintner's Quality Alliance), Canada's appellation system and pioneered the production of Icewine in Canada. He was awarded the Masi Civiltà del Vino Prize, one of the world's most prestigious winemaking awards. Both Ziraldo and Kaiser left Inniskillin in 2006.

Photo: Donald Ziraldo

MISTURA

an interview with Massimo Capra

What year did you open? What was your vision?

MC: We opened in 1997. The vision has changed a lot. Our idea was to do a cheap and cheerful, family-oriented, Italian-style trattoria. That didn't last very long. The demand from the public that was put on my partner and I meant we had to change. We're in a prime location, a destination location. This isn't the type of restaurant you stumble upon when walking down the street. This is a major thoroughfare. The people that come to our restaurant demand what we do best, which is a little bit high-end with better service and better food. I mean, cheap and cheerful is nice. I love it and I'm still chasing that dream, but this is why the vision changed.

It's now a high-end restaurant. When did that happen?

MC: The evolution happened within the first seven months of opening. We really started tweaking the menu, buying better linens, adding new wines, and getting better glasses and better cutlery. That was really our major change.

Did the menu change?

MC: Oh yes. The original menu was full of bruschetta and quick pastas and very inexpensive cuts of meats. It was all simply presented on platters—which is very different from what we do now. I don't like to overwork the food. I think that restaurants that are spending so much time decorating the plate are wasting their time. I think the food should be respected and presented in a more appropriate way. You can't fuss around too much on a plate. I prefer my food to be well prepared, cooked with the proper techniques and with the proper flavours, as opposed to being presented on a plate so that it makes a splash. I'm very old-fashioned that way.

Do you think simplicity and an emphasis on ingredients is a specifically Italian trait?

MC: I think that mentality plays a big role in my cuisine. As a matter of fact, I strictly use only all of the flavours you would find in Italy and I don't deviate from that at all. I know that there are a million restaurants that call themselves Italian and will do any combination of flavours, spices, and herbs. The more-the-merrier mentality is not what Italian food is about. It's about the simplicity of the flavours and the products that you buy. You don't cook with things that are out of season or not good to eat because that's when you get the most flavour. If I'm selling a fish I want the people to taste the fish. That's my idea. I know that's against the grain because people want a lot of sauce or they want to eat fish but they don't like fish and want to hide the flavour. There is a craziness about food in North America that is unbelievable. We work it through and we try to make the best of it. I believe that a little veal scaloppina with a little sauce and a small salad is heaven. I don't need to put a million things on it to make it better.

Do you think there has been an evolution in the mentality of the public in the last ten years? Is there more awareness of food that is authentically Italian?

MC: That's a loaded question. The public does know a lot more. The problem is that they know a lot more but they understand very little. Italy is not a place where you can say there is one general cuisine. What is Italian food to one person is different than what it is to another person. I come from the north in Cremona. In my parts, butter and animal fats are kings. We don't have any olive trees so we only cook with what we have. We don't eat fish. If you are by the coast in Italy you eat fish but if you are inland you eat meat. If you are in the south you eat a lot of olive oil and greens. In the north you might be hard-pressed to find that. If you go to Friuli, for example, you might find a lot of horseradish. But if you show horseradish to someone from Calabria they might look at you like you are from another planet. People know a lot but they only know a lot about what is available here. The Italians here have developed their own cuisine and that's what people here know. We know burrata in Canada more than they know it in Italy. No one there knows what 'nduja sausage is outside of Calabria. In Toronto if you don't have 'nduja sausage you're not Italian. It's craziness.

How does this knowledge affect your business? Do you adjust your menu accordingly?

MC: No. We've been at Mistura for fifteen years and we have an enormous following. We were here before all of the regional craziness of Italian cuisines started happening. What we've imposed on our clientele here is a broader Italian menu. What started happening over the past fifteen years is that half of my menu has become classic: if I remove any of those items I'll get lynched. I have to have certain things on the menu because it pleases my customers. I want to stay busy. It's a question of balance. The other half of the menu is seasonal and it changes every three to four weeks. We try to stay as seasonal and local as possible. If it can also be organic that's a bonus. I cannot even think of eating a tomato out of season. I go wacko. Why would I want to eat a tomato in January? I want to have cabbage soup in January. That's logical. But we have customers coming in from all over the world and if they want a bowl of raspberries in January I have to have them. We are very conscious about the local products and the seasonal products. But I sell everything if it's good.

Which ingredients do you import from Italy?

MC: I will not compromise on prosciutto crudo, parmigiano reggiano, gorgonzola, marscarpone or any of the cheeses. The ricotta is just about the only thing that I buy from here because it makes no difference. There are some local producers here of stracchino, which is one of my favourite little cheeses, and I have to admit that it is very good. One of the biggest shocks to me coming from Cremona was seeing the ground parmesan. I thought it was disgusting. I always used parmigiano reggiano and the consortium should really fight back.

How has the availability of imported products changed since you first opened?

MC: Products have always been available. I arrived in 1982 so I was really on the cusp of the explosion of Italian cuisine in Toronto. It was a little bit difficult to get the products and it was also very expensive. I arrived at a good time, though. I was working at two of the restaurants owned by my mother's cousin. They were French restaurants so I didn't need Italian products there. Personally, I would go to St. Clair and try and buy some of the stuff and it was really expensive. When my parents came to visit they would also bring me some products from home. Provolone was my favourite cheese and I wanted all of the trimmings.

Did working in French restaurants contribute to your technique or perception of how to do things?

MC: It was an eye-opening experience. In Italy restaurants are not that busy and do not function the way that they do here. Here they are open from 5:30 until 11:00. In Italy you open at 7:00 and close at 10:30. I came from a luxury hotel background. I worked in Milan, Courmayeur, Marina di Carrara, San Martino di Castrozza, and many other places. Normally service is two hours in Italy; here it is a different business. You sweat. It's really tough.

Describe your kitchen.

MC: I have seven guys in my kitchen and they really work hard. I supervise. It's a different way of doing business. People here want to eat too fast. In a proper restaurant in Italy you're there for the night: three hours. And here they give you big portions. When I arrived a 14-ounce prime rib was the norm. And that comes with potatoes and then people are

ordering salad and soups for their appetizers and I thought it was crazy. How do people eat this much? It's incredible!

For Italians eating is a ritual. How do you adapt the ritual to this market and still offer something authentically Italian?

MC: There are some techniques that I've implemented that I learned at fairs when I was working in Verona and Milan. There are things that can be done. When I arrived here in 1982 there were no handmade gnocchi on any menu. They gave you those rubber bullets that sit on a shelf in the supermarket. They're made with rice flour so they don't spoil. No one made agnolotti, tortellini, or risotto from scratch. Risotto was a big deal: you would have to call and pre-order it for two people the day before. There are restaurants in Milan and Rome where businessmen in suits eat and are out in 45 minutes or one hour. There are techniques you can use. You can order a beautiful risotto in Milan the same day and it tastes great.

There was a group of Italian chefs that arrived here in the 70s and we all learned those techniques in Italy. In those days in Italy the big brigades of twenty or thirty cooks in a kitchen were starting to shrink. You had to learn techniques to speed up the process. I will only put a pasta on the menu that can cook in four to five minutes, like spaghettini which are very thin. A twelve-minute spaghetti will take too long to cook. I have to serve the food within a ten to fifteen minute window. I adapt myself in order to do a proper job without compromising quality.

Let's talk about regional traditions. Is there anything really regional you have incorporated into your menu?

MC: Of course. There are many recipes from Cremona and Parma and Emilia. I import my own mostarda di Cremona from a great producer in that area and I use it for my duck preparation. The duck we do is a Cremonese style, more or less. But we do use some French and Canadian techniques when cooking it. Canadians like their duck breast undercooked and, quite frankly, I like the way that we cook meat on this side of the ocean as opposed to the other side. I find that it's too dry there. I make rabbit. I make lots of polenta. I make the proper Bolognese without the oregano in it. That drives me nuts when I see that! I freak out. I make lasagna with the proper sauce and the béchamel and all of that. A lot of people really like it and they ask, "Where's the mozzarella?" That's not proper lasagna. So I do the mostarda di Cremona, the polipo misto, beautiful frittata, and a lot of the cookies and many other things.

In your opinion, what makes Italian food so appealing and so universally appreciated? It's difficult to find someone who dislikes Italian food.

MC: I think that the genius of Italian cuisine is that you can be very picky about the product quality. You are altering it as little as possible and doing very appropriate combinations of flavours. I'm a big fan of Asian cuisine. I absolutely adore Chinese and Indian food but I find that the spicing is what takes over the entire dish. Maybe it's a function of the types of food that are available in those countries. In Italy we are very specific: every valley and plain has a specific food that they eat and the people are very focused on creating beautiful, quality products. When you have beautiful, quality products it's very easy to please the palate. When people taste Italian cuisine they may not understand why they love it but I firmly believe it's because of the simplicity and the quality of the ingredients that are used.

If you go to a restaurant outside of Italy and they use good quality ingredients from Italy, it tastes great, but if they do not it falls off the edge really fast. I heard one of my favourite chefs, Anthony

Bourdain, who was in Paris, say that the quality of produce in Europe in general is way better than what we have here. He's so right. Whether it's a little piece of lettuce or a squash it just tastes different. The flavour is superb. I don't know if it's because of the transport times. I go to California often and the produce there is quite good but once you get out of California it's like plastic. The best line from Anthony Bourdain is, "We have mountains and plains and valleys in America but the food just tastes different. Maybe it's because we're missing a couple of dead Romans." He's probably right. I don't know. My mom would go crazy in Italy to make sure that she bought the apples only from a specific farm. We don't have that option here.

You see a lot of chefs returning to tradition, others embrace fusion. How is Italian cooking evolving in light of these two trends?

MC: I think that fusion is inevitable here in Canada. In Italy, they embrace flavours a little bit more and are very specific. The Italians in Italy are less fearful of change than those here. They are interested in trying new flavours. But here, fusion is inevitable and it's a beautiful thing. I've had some amazing fusion meals. There is also a group of young chefs that want to go back and discover tradition. They're doing remarkable things, things that I've never seen. I only know the traditions of my region but not of other Italian regions. My upbringing will bring me back to the cuisine of Cremona, but I cannot cook Pugliese or Sicilian cuisine. The beauty is that I see a lot of different things from Italy being presented in a very beautiful and traditional way. There is space for that here more than in Italy. When I go to Italy I only eat at the trattorie. If I see something on the menu that does not belong to that region of Italy, I won't walk in; for example, tagliatelle bolognese in Cremona. I know that they aren't doing the right thing.

Is there anything you long for?

MC: The only thing that we cannot get here is a good tasting Italian prosciutto or salame or any of the cold cuts. They're getting better but I think the vacuum packing just kills the flavour of a lot of the meats that come from Italy. My mother brought me one wedge of parmigiano reggiano from the place where my great-grandfather used to buy it. That night, we opened it up and ate chunks of it and it was delicious. The next day we took it out of the fridge to make some pasta and the flavour had changed. It wasn't good anymore. I don't know what it is.

What do you miss about the culture or the way of being in Italy?

MC: Aside from some of the food products the biggest thing that I miss is the piazza or the bar where everyone meets. You just walk in. Whoever is there is there and you just chat. And then you ask, "Does anyone want to go for dinner?" And then everyone goes. That's what I'm missing. I don't understand how a city this big doesn't have a piazza. I miss Italian social life. I can't seem to find it here. You have to make dates with people to meet. You can't just walk in somewhere. It drives me nuts.

What is your favourite dish?

MC: Oh my God. There are so many. If I have to name my personal favourite, it has to be a pork or chicken cutlet alla milanese. That's my passion. I love that.

And the signature dish of Mistura?

MC: The signature dish of Mistura would be the red beet risotto. Fifteen years ago it was laughed at by the Italian Rice Federation judges, but now if you do a search for it on the internet, everyone makes it.

LA PALOMA

1357 St Clair Ave. W.

Owned: Mel and Salvatore Giannone

Opened: 1967

Highlights: gelato—fig, persimmon, and cassata siciliana are just some of the flavours, as well as soya cioccolato and frutti di bosco yoghurt.

Photo: Deborah Verginella

NOCE

an interview with Guido Saldini

When did you arrive in Toronto?

GS: I came from Milan in 1969. My ex-wife and I started a coffee house with my father-in-law in Yorkville at the end of the 1960s called Joso's. When we opened Joso's we were basically the only fish restaurant in town. It took awhile to establish ourselves. When we started serving octopus people were mind-boggled. Sometimes we had to cover it up because people would start screaming. I still remember when the first radicchio came to Canada. Before you could never find it and now everybody goes crazy for it. In the beginning, only a few people from Calabria and Puglia cooked with rapini but now rapini is everywhere; you have to have rapini in your restaurant.

When did you open Noce?

GS: Twenty years ago.

But you weren't in the restaurant business when you were in Italy? How did you learn?

GS: No, absolutely not. I came from a family that always ate well. The rest is just circumstance in life. We started with very old cooking and then, little by little, I learned to improve. It sounds very simple but it does take time. I don't claim to be a major chef. I've been in the kitchen for years and years. I actually went to university for philosophy and literature.

So you taught yourself?

GS: Yes, I taught myself. I was lucky because competition was very scarce. I never dreamed of doing this in Milan.

You talked about how people weren't familiar with certain products and then suddenly everyone wanted them. How did you work with that?

GS: Well, you introduce those products into a dish. When people like them they will ask for them, and then more and more restaurants jump on it. The city can be very finicky. I remember everyone used to go crazy for cigars. People from Bay Street would come, eat, and close deals and want to smoke cigars. Of course, after they smoked them they would throw up in the street but they had to have them! Everything is like that in this city. The same thing happened with balsamic vinegar. We never had real balsamic vinegar in this city. Why? Because everyone wanted balsamic vinegar but they didn't want to pay for real balsamic vinegar. But, little by little, we have come a long way.

Do you think your restaurant played an avant-garde role in that sense?

GS: Not now. Not lately. In the mid-1980s I opened a restaurant at Bay and Bloor called Carbonai. I know that thirty-five years ago, I was the first one to sell carpaccio. When I opened Carbonai I had to change the by-law to have a wood-burning pizza oven because I was the first one in Ontario to have one. Then I went back to Italy for a while. When I came back, I opened Noce. That was about twenty years ago. Then two years ago we opened Aria, close to the Air Canada Centre.

You have to evolve. This is not really a city where you can impose things. I just got a private shipment of passata di pomodoro one week ago, from Pachino in Sicily, and it is to die for. It costs an arm and a leg but nothing can come close to it in Canada because of the weather and the soil here. There is nothing that comes close to the quality of the cheeses that come from Italy. Now we have a guy that does the salting of our cheeses that come from Italy. We've had a business here for forty-two years. When I started it was impossible to have decent rice. It was impossible to have dry porcini. When I opened my first place I remember in the beginning we used to go through thirty-five pounds per month of fried calamari. Then we reached a peak of 1,200 pounds per month.

So how have things improved?

GS: The city evolved enormously thanks to importing. Everyone thinks Italian cooking is simple

and easy—simple because you use few ingredients. But the problem is that those ingredients need to be perfect. That's why you always try to import certain important ingredients. The improvement in this city has been enormous in the past thirty years. It's day and night. In fact, Toronto became one of the best cities in North America in which to dine out.

In New York, you can manage because you have flights coming in with fresh products daily from Italy but then you need the New York wallet to pay for it. Now, with niche importing you have the possibility to have some excellent niche products that are top of the line even in Italy. An example of this would be the cheese that comes from Piemonte. It is one of the top three cheeses in Italy, if not the number one cheese. We can get those cheeses here now but we were not able to just a few years ago. My olive oil for example, is something that I buy myself in small parcels in Italy because unless I want to pay $30.00 a litre everything else the market offers me is a fraud. Whenever you see olive oil for $7.00 here it is not real, because the cheapest olive oil you can get in Italy costs 14€. Whatever comes here was bottled in Italy but the actual oil comes from Turkey and all over. It's not that Turkey doesn't have good olive oil, but that's not what you're selling. Italy exports to the entire European community.

People who manufacture here have improved a lot, but again, it has to do with the raw materials they start with. They have to work with what they have. The seasons are what they are. They say to use local produce, but what is local produce? I would love to use local produce, but give me some flavour! Yes, fruits and vegetables are available twelve months of the year, but they have no flavour because they're coming from all over. In order to come from all over they are picked when they are not ready.

Do you think that Toronto today has a better understanding of what authentic Italian food is?

GS: A small percentage. The people who travel do. With the rest, it's impossible. If all of your life you've grown up with bad mozzarella, that is mozzarella for you; you don't know the difference. I remember when the first mozzarella di bufala came in—that took right away. The same thing is happening now with burrata.

Is there a difference between an Italian and a North American client dining in your restaurant?

GS: Do you want me to be honest?

Yes.

GS: Yes and no. If it's a North American that has been exposed to the real thing, he can detect the difference. If you've only been exposed to bad wine, it takes time to understand good wine. It's the same thing with food. Many of the Italian immigrants who came here were leaving poverty. They weren't coming from places where there was haute cuisine. They had excellent artisanal products but they didn't really know anything else. Here's the best example: I always kept a house in Isola d'Elba. It's a very small island, but there is a mountain. I met people living in one of the little villages on the mountain who only visited the city twice in their lifetime for a funeral. It has nothing to do with the culture. I have clients that are not of Italian background and know Italy better than I know it, and I am there every two to three months to visit my family.

What does it take for a restaurant to make it through tough times and deal with competition? There is a lot of competition for Italian food in this city.

GS: So-called Italian food. The reality of this business is that we are in the service industry. I'm not saying that we need to be the servant of anybody. I tell the people who work for me that when a party of four comes in here for dinner, the money that party spends here could easily feed that family for three weeks. We have to keep that in mind. As long as the customer isn't rude or acts out of place he is the one that pays your bills, your salary, and your rent. When you go shopping somewhere you expect to be treated decently. I think that's being polite. When people go out for dinner they don't want to hear about your problems. A lot of the time they are going out to escape their own problems and not to be bothered. I tell all of my workers to always smile. That's the name of the game.

How much of what you use is imported?

GS: I always try to buy the best ingredients. If it's not fresh pasta, I make my own. The dry pasta is imported. Whatever is a specialty is also imported, so capers, olives, olive oil, and tomatoes. My philosophy is always to buy the top products. Some people say I am just wasting money because ten or fifteen people won't even know the difference, but if only three people know the difference, that is good enough for me. They appreciate that these products are available to them. I will never move away from that.

How would you describe your menu? Is it traditionally Italian?

GS: Italian cuisine is so vast and enormous. You can change the presentation and the look, but the combination of ingredients has been the same since probably the fifteenth century. Some people say, "Why are you cooking with ginger?" Ginger has been used in Italy since the seventeenth century. I'm not putting in anything new. It's just that it hasn't been used a lot and now it is coming back. I didn't invent that. Not really. A person like Gianfranco Vissani was lucky because he was fighting with D'Alema, who was then the Prime Minister, and he was put on the map because of that. As a chef, he was great in presenting dishes. But the ingredients were there before him; he didn't invent those. The focus is on the freshness and quality of the ingredients.

Do you highlight a particular region at your restaurant?

GS: I try to stay away from that personally because I come from Milan. Milan has a poor cuisine. Immigration has not helped that. If you go to Milan it is very difficult to find a restaurant serving Milanese food.

What would be a typical Milanese dish?

GS: I don't know. Even to just get an osso buco or risotto alla Milanese in Milan is very difficult. It's not that you can't find it. It's that it's not made well or traditionally.

So you avoid regional foods?

GS: There will always be regional dishes on our menu but from different regions. I stay away from picking just one region. The menu changes a lot. There are more dishes from northern and central Italy than from the south but for economical reasons. You adapt. I don't like to be branded a regional cook. I always try to buy Ontario beef, lamb, and pork. It's very good.

What does it take to become a good chef in Italian cuisine?

GS: What I always suggest is to get a job, even a minimum wage job, working at a restaurant in Italy after you finish your schooling. Right now, two of my chefs are in Italy. I paid for them to go to learn. Only then can you acquire the taste for the real thing

so that you can duplicate it or come close to it. Otherwise there are certain things that you cannot describe, like the difference between basilico from Sardegna and Liguria, and why the one from Liguria is used to make pesto. Every small town has a different salame because they have different pigs that feed on different soil. This means there is a difference in taste.

Tell me about your new place, Aria.

GS: Well, we had some very good customers from Telus. They came to Elena and I with a blueprint for a restaurant in that building. It's a very good location, especially because they're building all around it. The building has major companies and is solid financially, but it was a difficult task. A Canadian architect did all of the woodwork and it is fantastic. The business is great there.

How important is the design and ambiance of a restaurant in terms of its success? Fine dining is more than just eating for the sake of eating.

GS: Right. It's more. Noce was about the quality of the food and the destination. Years ago we had to argue with prostitutes, pushers, and pimps. That's, of course, why the lease was good. The building is old so we couldn't do much inside. We had to make it cozy. We've always spent money. We spent $300,000 on the bar because it has temperature and humidity control.

Aria is totally different because it is completely modern. There we also spent a lot of money. It's a combination. There are examples of places in the city where millions are spent on décor, like we did, but the food isn't good. All you need is to disappoint a few people before the word goes around. Then it's impossible to get it back. It's up to you to deliver first and then to maintain it. It's nice when you have a couple here on their honeymoon and then they come back together years later on a business trip. That helps build confidence because keeping consistency is one of the most difficult things. In the service industry you have to do your best to keep people happy. It's a combination of things. It's about the food, making sure people feel comfortable in their surroundings, or having a waiter that is pleasant but not over-intrusive. It's a difficult balance.

Is there anything you miss about Italy?

GS: Personally, I miss pre-Berlusconi Italy. Now you feel embarrassed to be Italian or to go to Italy. Everybody is a thief. Italy is the number one most corrupt country. We finally made it. This is not something to be proud of. I don't miss that. What I miss about Italy and Europe in general is that here I need to take a plane to go somewhere different. There, all I need is a car or even a taxi. If I have a house in Milan I can take a quick trip to Monza and see a different history. If I take a half-hour plane ride I can land in a place with a different language, cuisine, and fashion. That's the beauty of Europe.

What do you cherish about Canada?

GS: Canada is the country where, if by 5:00 p.m. you lose everything, you can go home and sleep and know that you can wake up the next day and do something about it. In most places in the world this would not happen. If you are a young couple raising a family, I think this is a nice and easy place to do that. It's peaceful. Yes, the air is polluted, but compared to where I come from it is not that bad. You only say that because when you go up north to Muskoka you fall asleep so easily because there is so much oxygen in the air. Still, here the air is fantastic. If I go to Milan I spend the first two days crying because my eyes are not used to that pollution. Here I smoke three packs of cigarettes a day, but in Milan I only smoke two so my lungs can get a break. And I mean, Milan is not Mexico City or Cairo.

PAGANELLI'S RISOTTERIA

an interview with Gabriele Paganelli

You opened in 1997. When did you come to Toronto and why?

GP: I made the decision to come to Toronto at the end of 1990. Two years earlier I had had an offer from someone to come and work here but I said, "No." Then I changed my mind. This someone was John Lettieri who was opening his first coffee shops. I came to work for him as a gastronomist, that is, to choose and prepare foods for supermarkets and big stores. But we were at least ten years ahead of what people could understand, so he changed his plan and opened the coffee shops. I helped him with that.

Were you a chef in Italy?

GP: I was considered a "gastronomo tecnico": I prepared foods to take away. We were making between 100 kilos and 400 kilos of lasagna every day. Even in this we were a little bit ahead of our time. That particular kitchen was working mostly with supermarkets. Everyday we had a twenty-four item menu. The lasagna, of course, had to be there every day, but the other items changed depending on the season and the ingredients available at the market.

Which city are you from?

GP: Ravenna.

You grew up in a region with very rich culinary traditions. Was cooking a passion from the start? Did you know you wanted to be a chef?

GP: At school I studied electronics because as a ten-year-old that was my passion. At twelve I built my first radio. I was going to school in Cesena, about thirty-five km from my town, and when I would come home from school in the afternoon there was no more food left. I came from a large family and everyone had eaten everything so I had to cook for myself.

How many brothers and sisters do you have?

GP: Nine. I am the second of nine. I had to start cooking for myself. That became my passion and

I would invite my friends over or cook dinner for my family when I had the chance. When I left the army I knew I wanted to do this and I was lucky that my parents bought a little restaurant on the beach and a supermarket. I was able to cook there. In our area we work seven days a week for six months of the year and the other six months we have nothing to do. One year I went to a lake, another year to a butcher, and I took some courses to teach in schools as well.

Emilia Romagna is known for its rich ingredients and cuisine. Were those traditions and those ingredients familiar here in 1997?

GP: In 1997 I opened this restaurant after I had left my first job. Once I had decided to stay I was constantly moving around: I would work at a restaurant

for one year and then move on to a new one. I went wherever there was an opening because I wanted to learn as much as possible so that when I opened my own restaurant, I would make as few mistakes as possible. When I opened this restaurant I put out a simple menu people could understand. I had simple pastas that people were familiar with.

For example?

GP: Fettuccine alfredo, cutlets, pasta with tomato sauce. That was what the menu on the door offered, but if you came inside we would suggest personal favourites, like risotto. We have won competitions for the best risotto in North America. We also had pork meat, and donkey meat, and ravioli burro e salvia, which is a very simple dish, but until they tried it people, didn't understand it.

How long did it take Toronto to understand the simplicity of this cooking?

GP: They still don't understand. Last year I took sixteen of my customers around Emilia Romagna and Toscana. We went to all of the places that produce parmigiano, aceto balsamico and different cheeses. I cooked for them in a friend's house and when we came back they told me, "Now we understand what you are trying to do here." Even if they had been to Italy and Europe before, they hadn't understood. When I was in Italy I was trying to cook more than the traditional—something international. As a human being, we have the expression "L'erba del vicino e' sempre piu' verde." We always try to discover other things and learn. Now, even in Italy they are coming back to their traditions even if they do things like molecular gastronomy.

How would you characterize the food you create and the food from your region?

GP: I think the food from the region where I am

from is a little bit like Tuscan cooking. It is very simple. When there are only a few ingredients in a dish you understand those flavours right away. When there are too many ingredients in a dish you don't understand the flavours anymore. When you go there and eat at a restaurant in the mountains, it is good. Like the differences between wines from the New World and the Old World. If you drink wine from the New World it is easier for you to understand the flavours than if you were to drink the wines from Italy, France, or Spain. They are more complex and difficult to understand.

Do you see your food as being easy for people to appreciate, but difficult to cook because it is time-consuming?

GP: No, I think today, you can make tagliatelle more easily with a rolling pin than you could twenty or thirty years ago. My mom was making pasta or gnocchi at least two or three times a week because she had young kids and she had lots of stuff to do. I think that the food from my region is very simple to make and is even simpler to make today: we have machines that make the pasta and big refrigerators. Years ago ragù had to cook for three or four hours because the meat came from an old cow. The meat was dry and needed to be cooked for a long time to make sure it was safe to eat. Today we cook the meat sauce a lot less because the meat we use has less flavour and we want to keep the flavour inside the sauce. If people who are not a part of the culture come here, they can do some cooking classes and learn. It is fun for them because when they see how simple it is, they understand that they can do this for themselves at home. If I teach them how to make a tortellino it is simpler than if I teach them how to make a garganello.

How do you feel about the current emphasis on local or organic products? Is this a philosophy that originated from restaurants and chefs or is it the other way around?

GP: I think cooking what we have around is always the best thing. If I am cooking with a tomato that came from Mexico, it was picked at least 15 days before. When it comes here it has no flavour. A few years ago, I had some guests here from Sicily. I showed them all of the ingredients that we had and when we got to the pomodorini di Pachino, he said he was surprised we had those tomatoes: it was January and it was 10 or 15 degrees below zero. Obviously you cannot grow tomatoes here at that temperature. Sometimes it can be very difficult to reproduce the flavour. But going back to the original question, using the local products is always the best thing.

You are trying to preserve certain aspects of a tradition and communicate it to people here. What have you gotten as a chef and as a person from being in Toronto and Canada?

GP: Moving here from Italy I began to appreciate that I wasn't going to have a very good tomato or a very good lettuce, like radicchio. For years what was here was not really radicchio. When I came I had to make my own sauces, my own pancetta (which was more fun and challenging). It brought me back to when I was a kid and we used to make and preserve meat and tomatoes for the winter. It brought me back something that I had lost.

You've received the Marchio Ospitalità Italiana as well as numerous other awards. In terms of your tradition and experience, how do you understand hospitality?

GP: Hospitality is my job. Before I cook I am hosting the people that come in. Hosting is a very difficult thing and you have to love it, otherwise people will know you are not a good host and won't come back. I think I come from a part of Italy where we have that in our blood. The coast of that area saw a lot of Germans coming for holidays many years ago. So I think we became good at hosting people and you need to have that in you.

Do you think that coming from a large family also helped in forming the host in you?

GP: It is something that I learned from my parents too, because they are the ones who educated me.

You teach at George Brown. Do you concentrate on the cooking of Emilia Romagna?

GP: At George Brown there is a program where we teach certain regions. Italy doesn't have only one cuisine. It has twenty cuisines. It's a thirteen or fourteen week program where we teach regions that are close together. For example, Veneto and Friuli Venezia Giulia are together, Piemonte and Valle d'Aosta are also together. We have divided Italy into more or less 13 different regions. We have two teachers teaching seven weeks each. The

recipes I teach are my recipes, not the school's recipes or the government's. Every region of Italy has a different type of pasta so we teach them how to make pasta. If you go down from my region to the Marche or Campania or Calabria or Sicilia, the way they make pasta is very different. In my classes I teach six ways to fry because frying is the best way to cook. I learned that in one of the classes that I took. If you fry something like a potato at a certain temperature a chemical reaction takes place inside the potato. The insides of the potato are steaming and this keeps all of the vitamins and flavours inside the potato.

Which region has your favourite cuisine? Besides yours, of course.

GP: I don't know. I don't think that I have a favourite region after mine because all of Italy's cuisines are fascinating. I teach my students that what you put in your mouth is part of someone's culture. It is something that came together because it was a necessity.

In Italian culture sitting down at the table is a ritual, a moment of pleasure, of companionship. Is it possible to incorporate these aspects into your own restaurant with the fast-paced life of North America?

GP: Ninety percent, no. It's possible when you organize something for a small group of people and you try to transfer that kind of culture to them. Here everything is fast and we don't think about eating in that way.

In the last few years there has been an invasion of Italian restaurants and people are increasingly familiar with Italian food. How difficult is it to be competitive in this market when you offer a very specific type of cuisine?

GP: It is difficult. The customer, in general, doesn't understand what the real thing is. There are restaurants that are not really Italian and they take away the customers. This is part of competition and the rule of the market. You always have to be ready for this and try to be ahead of it. Usually, when you are the first to do something you are never the winner. I am opening another restaurant outside of town, in Bolton, where there is not as much competition. I will have more or less the same menu. Because it's outside of town where there are young people, I am incorporating other things that young people like. The place is big so I will do a lot of volume, but it is also the concept I came here with in the beginning. There are a lot of young people there that just want to eat and then go home so we try to encourage them to order before 3:00 p.m. so when they get home, they can pick up the food, go home and serve it.

Your signature dish is risotto?

GP: Yes, specifically the one served inside a parmigiano wheel with mushrooms. The risotto that won the competition has pheasant ragù and truffles. Sometimes I go to New York and San Francisco food shows to make this kind of risotto.

What is the ingredient you cannot do without?

GP: Flour. It is the basis of all of the regional cuisines of Italy.

Is it possible for an Italian-Canadian to learn how to cook the foods from your region?

GP: Yes, I believe so. You have to change the mentality of the students. It takes time. After the students finish the program they go for a semester in Italy. I always tell them to forget about the techniques and to pay attention to the flavours. There are flavours there that you cannot experience here. The techniques you can learn everywhere but the flavours can only be learned over there.

JAN K. OVERWEEL AND EMMA FOOD IMPORTERS

an interview with Pat and Arthur Pelliccione Sr.

Where were you born?

AP: I was born in Abruzzi in the province of L'Aquila.

What types of Italian products were available when you arrived?

AP: There was very little available in 1951. There was basic pasta, a little bit of olive oil, tomatoes, and some cold cuts.

How did the idea for your business begin?

AP: It was more of an accident than anything else. I was working as a butcher for a grocery store. I had just gotten married and somebody asked me if I would be interested in being a salesman for Italian food products. I liked what I was doing but it was not good for my health. I had rheumatism in my hands. I thought I would give it a try. The company that approached me was Primo Foods. At that time they were just in the meat and Italian-style cookie business and then they got into the pasta business.

Shortly after that I was asked to be the sales manager and then I became the general manager and eventually I took over the company. I was running it. The owner was semi-retired.

I expanded the line of Italian foods that we felt were suitable for the North American market. We went from importing to manufacturing and distribution. We had sales and distribution all across Canada. Then we started to export to the United States. When I started there were twenty-five people in the company. It grew to a company of over 1000 people. I was a shareholder of the company but we grew to the point that we were too large to be independent. When the owner died, the trust company sold the company and I sold my shares as well. I remained for three more years. That's where I got all of my experience in the food industry. I was there for approximately thirty years.

After that we had a company called Colombo Importing which imported mainly cheese. I was selling the cheese to Primo at the same cost that it came in because I had a conflict of interest with the people who bought Primo. I kept waiting to see what my family decided to do and fortunately, after they finished

school and gained experience in other businesses, they came back into the food business. We bought several food companies that sold mainly cheese because that was the base of our own company. Then we started to move into other sectors. At that time we were involved only in selling but now we're also involved in manufacturing as well as other joint ventures.

Cheese is the starting point of this company and you obviously you took a risk: was there a demand for it?

AP: Demand works in two ways. There is a natural demand and the demand you create based on what you're willing and able to do. If you're willing to take risks and expand the market and promote certain types of cheeses the demand will increase.

PP: To put it simply, what my dad's generation did was create products that satisfied the Italian palate from the 60s into the 80s. Then came globalization. There was a big difference between the products here and similar products in Italy. In 1991 until today we travelled throughout the world. We brought cheeses back from Italy, from Argentina, etc. The first ones were Reggiano, Parmigiano, Padano, and Pecorino Romano. In 1996 or 1997 we started bringing in these thirty-four kilo wheels of Parmigiano and we thought, "What are we going to do with them? How will we bring them to the stores? Will the shopkeepers know what to do with them?" Canadian parmesan was almost half the price of the imported one. But it was being used for ingredients. So we made friends with the shopkeepers and showed them our techniques and shared our sales expertise. We sent representatives to teach them how to cut, merchandise and promote them. Globalization really helped. Then you had the help of all of the cooking shows.

AP: The restaurants really helped us. They were the ones that we convinced to feature the products.

PP: Franco Prevedello was the leader. I remember being a kid in university and working at Primo and my buddy saying, "Come, I'm going to take you to an icon in this industry. He knows his stuff." So we went down to Centro with a bag of Lavazza coffee, then an up-and-coming brand in Italy. We brought it to Frank and he sniffed it through the hole. He said he would try it and give us his opinion. Today it's one of the leading brands worldwide.

That was around 1986. Before that, espresso coffee was brewed from the beans they roasted here. Italians had gotten used to that taste. It was an innovation. We took a chance.

AP: Another factor besides the help of restaurateurs was that people started travelling. They were exposed to real Italian food and wine. When they returned they looked for those products and recipes. That's why we put recipe books together. What was good ten years ago might not be today; you have to evolve. Today the Food Network is on all day long. Those recipes are very basic and easy to prepare. All of these things helped the Italian food industry.

What are the trends you are promoting today?

PP: There's the whole slow food movement. People want to get back to basics and use cleaner and more organic ingredients. That's where the market is going but the problems are ones not only of cost, but of time. I mean, everyone can make salami, but what we can do differently with that salami? Use less sodium, less nitrates, natural casings, etc.? We have to differentiate ourselves. Doctors are telling us to eat healthier, people are living longer, and we have to take this all into consideration. Italians have naturally had that Mediterranean diet. These imported organic products are very costly and some people don't want to pay for them, but that's the direction we are trying to go.

AP: There used to be this myth that Italian food was fattening. I had to fight that for over twenty years. We had to show people that the recommended portion of pasta is only seventy-two calories. It's what you add to it that's the problem. If you use excellent olive oil, low salt, good Italian tomatoes, and some basil, you have a good Italian product. These don't add calories. Now you might be up to 150 calories but you have a meal. It took years to get to that point.

When you started which product or ingredient was most requested?

AP: It was pasta and tomatoes. At the time we went to great lengths to improve the pasta made in Canada. It was made the way it was in Italy and the ingredients were pure, one hundred percent semolina. Today there are several imported pastas that people are accustomed to: if you give them bad pasta they won't buy it again. People know the product a lot better than they used to.

Both in terms of business and the culture you are promoting, do you prefer to import products or manufacture them here?

AP: We like to do both and I think there's a tremendous future for both. Our philosophy is to import products that cannot be imported in North America. They're very unique. For products that are in high demand we try to produce as much as we can in Canada. I know from experience you can make as good a prosciutto in Canada as you can in Italy. You just can't make prosciutto di Parma or San Daniele. We can come pretty close. Here we kill the pigs within six or seven months while in Italy they have to wait twelve or thirteen months. That gives you a different product, a different taste, and a different texture. I would say the good mortadella produced in Canada is as good as the one in Italy, if not better.

PP: Having said that, we import San Daniele and Parma prosciutto from Italy as well as Serrano and Iberico ham from Spain. We try to compliment the products we manufacture here.

AP: We're producing panettone now in Canada that is as good as the one in Italy. We have to put a lot of time, money, and research into it. We have to find the technology that will produce that result. That's what we're looking forward to this Christmas season. We always believe that quality will never be replaced with price.

I find that cheese in Canada is very expensive.

PP: Imported cheese is supply-managed by the government, that is, the amount of cheese that can be brought in is restricted. And this quota does not match the demand for the cheese: it's too small. This is one of the issues that drives up the price.

AP: It's supply and demand.

PP: We have mozzarella di bufala and burrata coming in every week from as far as Vancouver. Chefs want it. The servicing of this growing demand is made possible because of the frequency of air travel. We're able to move products frequently overnight into Germany or the Netherlands. We can have them over here in approximately twenty-four hours. You can buy whatever you want but you have to make sure that it's consistent with the quality. We have an army in charge of quality assurance.

We always say if we wouldn't feed the products to our children we won't buy them. You have to investigate the places you're buying from. That's why we travel so much. We like to interact with our customers. Our new centre in Montreal has a cooking facility there so chefs will come in and teach people how to use and cook with our products and we have staff that interact with salespeople overseas to make sure they understand the product.

AP: We go to great lengths to find out where the trends are going. That's why we attend every major food show in the world. People say, "Why are you going there? You already have all of your brands here!" And I say, "Well, it's a new city that I want to see." You see new products, new innovations, and new packaging methods.

This is a family business. Do you think future generations will work in this business and continue the success you have today?

AP: I learned one thing a long time ago. A man used to tell me, "Arthur, so you seed, so you reap." I

hope I've sown the right seed, and I think what I see around me is what I've done. It's up to them to do the right thing for the next generation. But it's more and more difficult with every generation.

PP: When you get big you need to find new ways to motivate people. We're still trying to run it like a small company but the structure makes it difficult to maintain that feeling. Structure is required for profitability but you still have to find a way to be creative. That is the challenge for the next generation. I have two boys. One will be fifteen this year and the other will be thirteen. I can't picture them sitting behind a desk or flying some place new every week. We'd like them to be here but whether or not they want to be here remains to be seen.

You need people that are effective. They need to have the qualifications and ability to manage and to help the company grow. The structure is very important when you get bigger.

AP: Remember, nothing is done without people. It's people. If you have the right people you're successful. You could be selling diamonds at a cheap price but you still won't be successful if you have the wrong people.

Is there a favourite family recipe?

AP: That varies. I always go back to the pasta dishes. I always enjoy it but only if I eat the right amount. If I eat too much of it, I don't enjoy it.

Whatever we manufacture or import you can pretty well make any dish and have it be a favourite dish. If you start with the right base and the right ingredients the quality will come through.

Do you miss anything about Italy?

AP: Of course, but I'm there about six times a year. My choice place to live is Canada.

PP: Not during the winter!

AP: I've been fortunate enough to travel the world but when I come back to Canada I say, "Thank you God." I like Italy and I enjoy it. I don't think there's an area of Italy that I don't like. But I'm glad I live in Canada.

MERCATTO

330 Bay St., 101 College St., 15 Toronto St.,
220 Yonge St., Eaton Centre

Owners: Jack and Domenic Scarangella

Opened: 1998

Menu Highlights: handmade, ricotta-filled ravioli with pine nuts, arugula and brown butter, cheese board, pizza

Fact: They pioneered the *Enomatic* wine preservation system where wines by the glass are portion, temperature and quality controlled for up to thirty days. Mercatto became the go-to place to sample unique varieties of Italian wines for institutions offering sommelier programmes. And all four locations have a BYOW (bring your own wine) licence.

Awards: Wine Spectator Award 2012 for their unique selection of wines.

PIZZERIA LIBRETTO AND ENOTECA SOCIALE

an interview with Max Rimaldi & Rocco Agostino

You opened Pizzeria Libretto in 2008 and introduced pizza napoletana to the city. Was that your aim?

MR: For me, it was very simple. I grew up right here at College and Ossington and I wanted a place in my area that I could go to on a regular basis that was cozy and didn't break the bank. Whenever I have an idea for a concept I then want to do it. I was a huge fan of pizza ever since I was a little kid. My mother made pizza at home. It's always been my favourite food from birth.

Is your family from Napoli?

MR: My family is originally from Frosinone, so halfway between Rome and Napoli. In my town they make a lot of wood-burning ovens. There's a factory. I decided on pizza napoletana because there's an incredible story behind it and its heritage. All pizza is great pizza to me, but this is the original pizza. That's where it was invented. We have to be true and authentic. I like to be as real and honest as possible. This is very real and very honest.

RA: I think our place really reflects the passion Neapolitans have for their pizza combined with the passion of wanting to have a neighbourhood restaurant that serves authentic food.

Where have you worked in the past?

MR: I worked for a group on King Street. I helped open up Brassai and the Brant House, more fine dining restaurants. I actually came from fine dining to do this. My first job was at Ciao Bella in Woodbridge and that's actually where Rocco and I first started working together. There, I would be walking with a million plates and the chef would just swear and yell, "Stop!" He felt he was always supposed to have the right of way. I got that, but there was no need for him to talk to me like I was a cockroach! With all the years I spent dealing with chefs and their big egos, I decided I would open up a restaurant and the only person I would open a restaurant with is Rocco. He's super talented and I knew I would only be able to open up a restaurant with someone that I get along with. Outside of here, we're friends. Our kids and wives hang out together. That always makes life easier.

What is your relationship with Italian food, Rocco?

RA: My parents are from Calabria. I've been cooking for about twenty-five years. I've always had a passion for cooking since I was young. As a teenager I would cook for my friends, but I didn't really take it seriously or consider it as a career until I was about twenty.

Where did you grow up?

RA: I grew up at Dufferin and Dupont and later, at Dufferin and Lawrence. I was at a point in my life where I didn't know what to do. I was sitting down at the dinner table with my family and I asked them what they thought of me going into cooking. My dad didn't really say much. My first job happened to be at Ciao Bella, then from there I went to chef's school and worked in Rome for about a year. I had my own restaurant for about ten years.

MR: Yeah, I worked with Rocco too at one point.

Where?

RA: At the Silver Spoon. Then Max came to me with his idea for the restaurant and the rest is history.

What makes your menu special? Can you describe it to me?

RA: Simplicity, honesty, and flavour. We're really just passionate about what we do and are honest about it.

MR: I'll give you a great example. I think every Italian restaurant on this earth has a caprese salad. We also have a caprese salad but it's in the summer when the tomatoes are fresh and at their peak. We use heirloom tomatoes, some mozzarella, olive oil, and a pinch of salt. In the winter we do a beet ca-

prese salad because we're not going to use tomatoes that have been refrigerated and flown in from around the world—they don't have flavour. We're an Italian restaurant and, specifically, a Neapolitan restaurant. Italian cuisine is very regional. But the point is that there's a lot of thought behind it. If you ask Rocco for a tomato salad in the winter, he will say no.

RA: That's just what Italians have done for ages. They take advantage of what's in season and use ingredients when they are at their peak.

How do you stay true to this in Canada, given what is in season? How much space is there for creativity?

RA: Well on our menu we have a pizza margherita and a marinara.

MR: Those are the only two pizzas recognized by the DOP as being authentic. I mean, if you tell someone you're putting duck confit on a pizza, they'll tell you you're crazy.

RA: We are crazy.

MR: But it's delicious! So there is room for creativity.

So on the one hand you are aiming for authenticity and on the other you want to create your own twist.

MR: Yes, there's a very basic secret behind the success. I don't know if we want to tell you … the secret is simple. We have a chef that puts together our pizzas. The big deal is that Rocco's duck confit pizza is duck confit made properly. It's cooked for just the right amount of time, it's cared for, and there is just the right amount of salt. That's something that only a good chef can do. A pizzaiolo might say that he or she can make that pizza. Try.

Try and make proper duck confit and pair it properly. It's all about restraint and the right amounts. The proper margherita for example, has to have exactly eighty grams of tomatoes and exactly eighty grams of mozzarella. There's a reason for that. You need a special hand for that. What makes us special is that we can do that because we have a trained chef who knows what he's doing.

You were trained and formed as a chef here.

RA: Yes, but I also went to Italy.

Was that essential for you to be able to cook authentically Italian food?

RA: My parents are from Calabria. I grew up in the kitchen watching my mom cook. It's in my blood. It's also passion. I wanted to go to Italy to understand why and how they did things. It's a combination of my education, my background, and my training abroad.

Can everyone appreciate food that is authentically Italian? Has it evolved over the past ten or twenty years?

MR: Definitely people understand more now, but this isn't true of everyone. A simple margherita made with four ingredients is not for everyone. They'll say, "$13.00 for this? I can make this at home or get a party size pizza for $20.00 that feeds my entire family." And that is true but that's the point: if you don't get it, you're never going to get it. We are very lucky in Toronto that our best-selling pizza is the margherita. I'm glad that people get the simplicity of it and the quality of the ingredients. It's a cosmopolitan city and people have great food knowledge.

If we tried to do this ten years ago, I'm not sure it would have worked. The three hour line up on Saturday nights is a testament to the maturity of the diners. Neapolitan pizza is just blowing up worldwide and diners understand that. It's not exactly the healthiest thing for you but it's cooked in its most pure form. Everything is fresh. I still have pizza every day after five years. I'm pretty healthy, I think.

Do you import most of your ingredients?

MR: Mozzarella is the key point for us. You can't touch mozzarella in Italy. It's the best. I was at a factory in Italy where they make fresh mozzarella and I took a bite out of it and I almost lost my mind—it was ridiculous! The problem with it is that it is highly perishable. I prefer to use something fresh produced here rather than flying something so perishable over and leaving a huge carbon footprint.

RA: We do source out as much local stuff as we can. The cheese is made here specifically for us. It's delivered three times a week, freshly made. The tomatoes come from Italy because I haven't found a comparable tomato here. We're sourcing the best ingredients: if they have to come from Italy, that's where we'll get them from.

Tell me the idea behind Enoteca Sociale.

MR: The idea again was to have a neighbourhood place you could eat a good bowl of pasta and drink a glass of wine without breaking the bank. We decided we needed to grow a little bit, to mature. Rocco is an incredibly talented chef and he needed to broaden his horizons. We wanted to make the menu the same format as the Silver Spoon. There's one fish, one poultry, a whole bunch of appetizers and pastas. The wine program is really important there: about 90% Italian, but the rest is local. There are Ontario wines on the list.

How Italian is your menu?

RA: It's a seasonal menu which, Luca, the chef there, changes based on the products coming in.

MR: He'll go to the terminal and bring back some ingredients and start creating new dishes. There are some staples on the menu like the bucatini all'amatriciana and the cacio e pepe. We don't want to touch those, but we do have a lot of fun with the pastas and appetizers. They're pretty creative and the menu does change pretty frequently.

What does it take to stay competitive among so many Italian restaurants in Toronto?

RA: For me, it's just dedication to the craft. As long as you stay true to that, you're good.

MR: This partnership is like this for a reason. I like to handle the business aspect and he likes to cook. I don't want him to worry about competition. We just focus on what we're doing here. On my end, I'm constantly looking at what's going on in the city but I don't want to lose focus of what's going on here. We were the first to say we're doing Neapolitan and not Italian. Now, there are a lot of pizzerias out there, they can only catch up. We just keep moving forward and doing our own thing. Our job is not just to put food and wine on the table, our job is to blow you away. That's the only thing we can do to stay competitive.

What do you embrace most about Italy and Italian food?

MR: I love the dedication to craft. The last time Rocco and I were in Italy together we would go out with his cousin, Rocco. We would have dinner, then a gelato, and finally an espresso. We would say, "Rocco, can't we have dinner and gelato here?" He would always tells us that you need to eat dinner at the best place, have gelato at the best place for gelato, and then have espresso at the place that makes the best espresso. Too bad if they're not all the same place. I need to concentrate on one thing and do it really, really well. That's what we do here. We do pizza. Could we offer entrees? Sure, but it takes away from how special the pizza is. That's what I take away from Italy. It's one guy doing one thing really well for his entire life, and then teaching his son how to do that, who teaches his son how to do that.

RA: Being a pizzaiolo there is what you do for life. That dedication gets me fired up but so do the ingredients. The tastes, smells, and sights are incredible. It just tastes better. For me, the challenge is trying to take that dish and bring it to Toronto and make it as authentic as possible. Again, we're not in Italy, so it's that dish as perfect as it can be, given the circumstances.

There are some new trends in Italy, perhaps an openness to other ingredients. Does that idea of (for lack of a better word) fusion appeal to you?

RA: I wouldn't use fusion. I do incorporate ingredients that aren't found in Italy but are found here in Toronto. I cook with an Italian philosophy.

MR: I'm open to trying new methods if they can be better, but sometimes it's really just reinventing the wheel. You can bring me a high-tech $50,000 oven, but nothing will replace the oven that we have downstairs which people have been making for over 150 years. There are no technological advancements in that oven. If you could make me a better pizza, then maybe I would try it out.

Are you inspired by other regions?

MR: I've loved southern Italian food up to this point but I'm really interested in food from the Alto-Adige and in northern cooking. Instead of olive oil, it's good butter or instead of pasta, it's a good risotto. But Rocco cooks the food, so it's really whatever drives him to love something.

RA: Each region in Italy has something special to offer. Alto-Adige is a great region that offers some pretty interesting dishes. The south is simple and great, but there are places like Sardegna that people don't always get to see much of. There is a lot of spectacular food in Italy.

Why did you choose the name "libretto"?

MR: "Libretto" means "little book." If you read the official rules for making a pizza that tell you exactly how many tomatoes to use and how long to cook it, they say that the sign of a proper Neapolitan pizza is to be able to take a slice and fold it al libretto, or "like a little book". That's the sign of quality.

Your favourite pizza or favourite creation?

RA: I do love our sausage pizza. The margherita is a classic.

What's your signature pizza?

RA: The margherita by far.

MR: The margherita is the benchmark. Everyone makes a margherita all around the world. I think Rocco's signature is the duck confit because it's so interesting and it makes a statement.

RA: We also went to Las Vegas and made a porchetta pizza with some truffle shavings and some rapini.

MR: I'm a margherita guy. I have a rating scale and I've never had a 10/10. I've had a 9.5/10 here and a 9.5/10 in Naples at Da Michele, but the margherita is definitely my go-to.

NOTA BENE

an interview with Franco Prevedello

Tell me about arriving in Canada from Italy.

FP: I come from a small town near Treviso in the north of Italy. I came to Canada in 1966 to work at Expo 67 in Montreal. I worked in Toronto for awhile before Expo. After that, I got married and moved to Florida for awhile. We moved back to Europe for a few months. And then I've spent most of my life—the past forty-five years—in Toronto.

Where did your interest in food and the restaurant business come from?

FP: I did some schooling in Italy. It was one of the most well-recognized and respected schools. It was an easy way for me to travel to Germany and to France. It was an excuse to get out of a small town and gave me the opportunity to travel through Europe in the post-war years. I learned the trade and I stayed in it for quite a while.

What was the Italian food scene like when you arrived? What kind of food was available?

FP: Italian food was College Street and St. Clair. The food was basically simple, very good and traditional food. The immigrants that were here from Italy were mostly from the south. But everything was limited. The Italian restaurants that were here at that time were not very well regarded because the French and Swiss chefs dominated the city. In the mid-1970s we had Vittorio's, Pronto, Biffi, and these were the restaurants that started off the so-called North Italian cuisine. The only reason we called it North Italian cuisine was to differentiate ourselves from the traditional maccarone, lasagna, and cannelloni, and so forth. That is all great food, but we wanted to do something a bit difficult. There were about two or three of us that did that. Then Centro and Splendido and Terra came along and there we did Italian cuisine that was adapted to the North American market.

How did you adapt it?

FP: I was following a lot of what was happening in California at restaurants like Spago. What these American chefs had done was adapt Italian cuisine to the North American system. For example, Wolfgang Puck at Spago in the 80s re-introduced pizza to America, but he made pizza with smoked salmon and smoked duck. It wasn't a pizzeria anymore. We did the same at Centro, Splendido, Acqua, and Terra. It was Italian food re-adapted to North American tastes. If you go to Italy today the cuisine is very regional. That's the beauty of Italian cuisine, but it was not easy to introduce regional cuisine here in the 80s, so you had to introduce something that would give it a little bit of an ambiance. It was Italy with a touch of California. We did very well with it. Italian restaurants are opening up every day. They are very present and predominant.

Did those restaurants usher in an era of more refined dining?

FP: Yes, it was a more fine dining experience with a bigger wine list. We were the first ones to bring in quality wines in the 80s. Before you had big brand name wines but the smaller Italian brand wines were brought in by the restaurants. I was at the forefront of that.

How did you know the moment was right? Were people ready for this?

FP: Absolutely. It took quite a bit of travelling but I was at the right age to do something fresh and new. When we opened Biffi on Mount Pleasant it was just a small little restaurant. There were line-ups all the time. It was the same with Centro, Splendido, and Bindi. They were very successful restaurants. Some of them are still around twenty-five or thirty years later.

What was your role in opening Centro?

FP: I'm a restaurateur so my task was to find the location. I opened Centro right after I came back from Expo '86 in Vancouver. I had to find the location, the right space, the décor, the menu, and the chef. I was the guy that did it all and I enjoyed all of the phases of it—not just running the restaurant, but building it and everything else. I thought it was time to express an Italian piazza more than just a little pizzeria. It was time to show that Italy was able to do better than just the average of what was served in those days.

Did the chefs you worked with come from Italy? Did you have any particular requirements in that sense?

FP: I chose top chefs. Some of the chefs were Italian. I would say Centro, Splendido, Terra, and Acqua saw some of the greatest chefs cook there. Some of them had an Italian background but I knew what I wanted. Even if the chef wasn't specifically Italian I knew what I wanted and would have him work with me to develop that product. When the possibility came, I definitely had Italian or Italian-trained chefs.

Each of those restaurants had their own identity. Did you focus on a specific target market or clientele when you opened those restaurants?

FP: Opening a restaurant is a little bit like theatre: you set a stage and people will come. I didn't have a specific target and I didn't do any market research, but I thought the timing was right and the product was right so people would come. Then we built up a great reputation so every time a new restaurant would open up, it became busy right away. I did that with a number of restaurants. I think right now it's time for Italian cuisine to re-establish itself in Toronto because it has gone sideways a little bit. It's not bad, but there is not, for example, a specific Italian restaurant. There are some, but they are older restaurants. There are few expressing the real feeling of Italy. There is a touch of Italy in every restaurant that opens right now because pasta and risotto are very prominent, but is there a specific Italian restaurant that makes you go 'wow'? I don't know.

What do you think is missing?

FP: You need somebody that is really focused on doing that type of cuisine and has the right talent to do it.

What trait of Italian food is a priority in your opinion?

FP: Ingredients are number one. Quality is very important. At one time restaurateurs could use the excuse that you didn't have access to the right ingredients in Canada. That's not true. We have great meat here and you can import a lot of great products from Italy. We have great fish and great bread.

How did the concepts change with each new restaurant you opened? Was it a progression?

FP: When you are young, you are restless. I opened up a new restaurant almost every year. It was something that I wanted to do. I never did a Centro 1, Centro 2, Centro 3 because I had done Centro. I loved creating and establishing restaurants. Then I would move on to something else. For me the concepts and building the restaurants were more important than the ownership of them.

Is there still a place for restaurants like Centro and Splendido in today's market of trattoria chains?

FP: Yes, there is still a place: Centro is changing its concept and name right now. It is twenty-five years old. I think there is space but you have to revisit the total market. It's like building a car. It doesn't work today, but to me, the concept was like a great Porsche. It's the same design but refined every year.

There is always a market as long as you keep the quality up. A restaurant can last forever or it can last six months, and not because it's good or bad, but because it's not innovative. Or you can try to appeal to a certain group of people, but then they get old and move to Florida.

What do you think of today's penchant in young chefs for incorporating foreign techniques and tastes into Italian cooking?

FP: That's the world today. Great chefs from Italy don't come over here every day. You have to take someone who has a passion for Italian food. A lot of these chefs have trained in Italy. You don't necessarily need to be Italian to cook Italian food well. In fact, I would say that the non-Italian chefs are more progressive than Italian chefs.

What do you think is the near-universal appeal of Italian food?

FP: Italian food has always been very approachable. There are other types of cuisines that are more demanding and more sophisticated but you can cook Italian food yourself at home or you can go to a restaurant. The ingredients are usually fresh and you rarely need to use many ingredients. If you go to a little trattoria or a big restaurant, the understanding is there. That's why there is such a presence of Italian restaurants. By being approachable Italian food can appeal to a large mass of people.

In your opinion is the food being offered here far from being authentically Italian?

FP: I think so. I think you need to be careful not to stray too far away from original recipes but, again, the new restaurants with young chefs are tending to stay very close to the mark. I've had some great restaurant meals cooked by young Canadian chefs and they go to Europe quite often.

So it can be reproduced?

FP: Absolutely. That's the beauty of it. If you wait for the Italian chefs to come here it won't happen. The best thing is to train your own local chefs and make sure they understand the ingredients we have here. I used to send young chefs from here to work with the best Italian chefs. Even in Italy there are people wandering away from Italian cuisine. What we are seeing here is more and more authentic Italian food and less of fusion cuisine.

What do you make of the trend of restaurateurs using only local or seasonal products?

FP: Local and fresh ingredients are important, but our seasons are very short here so you have to be careful when going local. We have great products in the summer and in the fall but then we have a long winter. You need to serve products that are available worldwide and try to maintain freshness. The climate restricts us here a little bit in terms of quality, but also in terms of what is available twelve months a year. The restaurant is open twelve months. You can't just close for six months because certain products are unavailable.

As a frequent traveler to Italy, do you see new trends in Italian cuisine that are being imported here?

FP: I think that everybody today is more conscious, not just of the beauty of food, but of the quality and freshness of food. If you have great fresh pasta, great tomatoes, and great basil that's all you need. With Italian food you don't really need more than three ingredients. Restaurants are changing in Italy and becoming more regional. They're trying to show that they can do one thing very well rather than trying to be everything to everybody. It's happening worldwide. I was just in California and the great restaurants have small and fresh menus, but they are very good menus. They're not trying to be something they're not because the clientele is very sophisticated today. It's important to be what you are. For example, the great trattorie with great service and great food are starting to come back again in Italy. For a while people went to high end restaurants but they are now realizing that they weren't as high end as they thought they were. That's what it's all about in Italy. It's not necessarily about going to a Michelin star restaurant because that's not our culture. Great, original, local food is our culture.

Which do you prefer?

FP: I'd go to a good restaurant. I would go to the three Michelin star restaurants just to see what they're doing but I can also get that food in New York or Miami. When food is being touched fifty times, I'm not interested in that: my interest is in the local product. If I go to Piemonte I will eat certain foods. If I go to Tuscany I will eat certain foods. I like to eat local cuisine which is well done. The young chefs are doing that more and more. It's the same thing in Toronto.

You've been in Canada for a number of years. Are there things that you miss about Italy?

FP: It's my home so I definitely do miss certain things but I am lucky enough to be able to go back three or four times a year. Part of my family is still there. I'm Italian and I love Italy, but I'm also Canadian and I love Canada. I've been here for forty-five years. The Italy of today is a different Italy than the Italy I left, partly for the better, but also for the worse. I hope that they find their way. Italy is not all dreams anymore. In the 1970s and 1980s maybe it was. There was happiness and simplicity. Today Europe has problems. I see it when I go back. People are not as happy as they used to be. Before they were more free-spirited but now there is a lot of tension there.

Cultures here can blend but certain communities can still maintain their own traditions.

FP: With the first generation, yes. With the next generations things will change. Canada is the filter between Europe and the United States but we are two generations away from becoming like the United States.

So the next generations will have less of a cultural understanding of Italy?

FP: Maybe not less, but a different understanding. It will not be the same as a first-generation understanding because we were born there. Second-generation Canadians are more Canadian. It's not to say that they don't appreciate Italian food, products, or fashion, but they are one generation detached. Two or three generations later, the melting pot comes in. They are Italian by name.

Do you have any future projects in the food industry? Is there anything you'd still like to accomplish?

FP: I'm doing a restaurant right now, but it's a bistro. I have two great partners who are not really trained in Italian food so we are doing what they are best at. The opportunity to do a great restaurant may come but I am very fussy about finding the right team. It's always in my mind, but we'll see.

Was there anything or anyone that inspired you to get into this business?

FP: I went to school in Italy just to get out and travel the world. It was a way for me to be able to get a job anywhere in Europe. I thought that if it would take being a cook or a manager, I would do it as long as I could travel. That's how it started.

Do you have a particularly memorable moment from your years in the restaurant business?

FP: I don't think I have a specific one. It's a combination of memories. The opening of restaurants is always special. It's like opening the stage of a theatre. The building of the restaurant also adds a special character to the whole process. Centro is maybe the restaurant that I was most satisfied with.

Where do you find gratification?

FP: It comes from many years of service. It's not the money that's important. Being successful means that you are creating something for the neighbourhood that is important to that neighbourhood. Restaurants tend to be very important to a neighbourhood. That's why I build different restaurants in different areas that are a little bit different to fit into those neighbourhoods.

Can you give me an example of two restaurants to illustrate how they fit into their respective neighbourhoods?

FP: Centro was North Toronto. It catered to a more downtown crowd. Acrobat was on Bloor Street and it was more hip and club-like. Acqua was very corporate because it was in a business district. Terra was a little bit of downtown to where it was in Richmond Hill. It depends where you are located.

What is your favourite dish?

FP: I'm a fan of risotto. It's a very difficult dish to do right.

What kind of risotto?

FP: Any type, but with white truffles specifically. We introduced risotto because it was not very well known here. People initially did not want to pay a lot for a bowl of rice, but once they understood how difficult it was to cook, they came around.

PIZZA NOVA

an interview with Domenic & Sam Primucci

You opened your first location in 1963. What was the state of pizza at the time?

SP: In 1963 there were very few pizza places in Toronto. Two come to mind: Totò Pizzeria at College and Euclid and Vesuvio at Dundas and Quebec Avenue. They made a very good product. Very similar to what we make today. Then people saw that the evolution of pizza was going to be a big thing so other places started opening. Totò Pizzeria and Vesuvio made sauce from plum tomatoes but the others used pureed tomatoes to camouflage the sauce. That's how the change started.

My brother Mike worked at a pizzeria at Bathurst and Lawrence which delivered to Scarborough, if you can appreciate that. There were no stop lights, traffic was fast, and even though it was so far away, it really wasn't that far away. He said, "We have to open something up in Scarborough." We opened our first location at Lawrence and Kennedy. One of our pizza makers who worked with us for twenty-five years (a former Fiorentina player) originally worked at Totò Pizzeria. And so, of course, we made sauce as it should be made and not with pureed tomatoes.

DP: It was authentic.

SP: Now, the area we delivered to was Don Mills which was built by E.P. Taylor. He came from one of the richest families in Canada. The area was a bit more affluent than our other area and they understood good food. That gave us the initiative to stay the course of quality. The customers demanded that. As other pizzerias opened the customers noticed a difference. We realized that you can't please everybody, but as long as you had 51% of the people, you were a winner. Our customers were very loyal.

DP: We stayed focused on what we were doing and what we did well. Instead of suddenly bringing in another menu item just to bring in another menu item to try and capture another portion of the food market, we focused on the pizza and the Italian food market. This is who we are as a company and we want to do it as best we can. We want to ensure we have a great product.

SP: For instance, we were the very first company to use only the centre cut of bacon and not the

ends which has a lot of fat. If you cut an inch and a half off each side of a strip of bacon, the middle is actual bacon and it tastes better. It may cost a little bit more money, but this is what we use. Another example is Spanish onions versus cooking onions: Spanish onions are triple the price of cooking onions and for fifty years we have only used Spanish onions.

You are using bacon, a Canadian product. How can you maintain what is authentically Italian and embrace what is Canadian, but still stay true to a tradition?

DP: A traditional pizza in Italy is the margherita pizza, a basic pizza without extra toppings. When you construct a building you need a strong foundation. In our products the foundation is the dough, sauce, and cheese, the basic margherita pizza. You have to have the best possible dough, a good sauce gives a lot of flavour, and then a great cheese is also important. From there you build based on what the customers want. We're not in an Italian market, we are in a Canadian market. People want authentic tastes so we have more gourmet toppings such as sun-dried tomatoes or bruschetta.

SP: Back in the day, whenever people wanted Italian food they bought it in a can, they bought Chef Boyardee. Then they realized that pizzerias make good spaghetti and meatballs and this ushered in the spaghetti and meatball era. From there menus changed and included saltimbocca alla romana, which restaurants don't even make today. It's something from the past. Eventually, the market realized that Italian food is not Chef Boyardee and it's not spaghetti and meatballs. It's a really good pizza or a really good saltimbocca alla romana or pasta with alfredo sauce. It's been an evolution and slowly the Canadian market discovered that Italian cuisine is more than just pizza. In Canada there are a lot of good pizzerias. We make better pizzas, believe it or not, than the commercial pizza in Italy that you might find at an autogrill. In Rome you have Pizza Chef, which has about ten or twelve locations, but it's terrible pizza. I think that we can be proud that we brought something to this country and we made it even better. The only difference between Italian pizza and Canadian pizza is that they have fresh ingredients and we don't. We have basilico that is refrigerated. They have basilico that they pick from the plant in the morning and then use to make pizza in the afternoon, so the taste is different. The freshness aspect of it really plays a big part.

What are some of the highlights of the last fifty years for Pizza Nova?

SP: We had a marketing day. In those days Honest Ed's used to have a dance marathon where people would win a lot of money, so we had one at Pizza Nova. We set up a stage and contestants got up and danced for two days and nights continuously. I think it was 1965 or 1966. That was really a thrill. It was a happy occasion because people really enjoyed themselves.

SP: Oh, yes, that was really memorable. About ten years ago, we wanted to see where Pizza Nova was headed, so we sat down and debated whether we wanted to be like everyone else or to differentiate ourselves. I really struggled with that. We decided to better ourselves. We talked to one of the top designers in the world, Diego Burdi, who studied under Yabu Pushelberg. He asked me, "Sam, are you sure that after forty years in this business that you want to change?" And I said, "Yes, I am." He said, "I don't believe you. Think about it. Every time we change a logo for a company they have a lot of problems accepting it." I said, "Diego are you trying to talk me out of it?" He said, "I'm just telling you the truth." I spoke to Domenic and we decided that we would go ahead and make the change. Diego prepared one hundred different sketches. He delivered us a pile and told us to take all the time in the world to look them over and to narrow it down to four or five. We could only save one. We met with Diego and his partner and showed him the one that we picked and he said, "Oh my God. Are you kidding me?" I said, "No." He looked at his partner and said, "Do you believe these two guys?" We had picked the one that they had also chosen. Then they told us to go home and sleep on it.

DP: We believed in it. You have to believe in what you're going to do to move forward. We believed this was going to take our company to another level.

SP: We increased every location by 30% because of the rebranding and the remodelling. Our store at Lawrence and Yonge Street is in a very affluent area. We wanted to change the sign there to see how people would react; we changed it ten or twelve times. The colour of the green wasn't quite right so

we kept changing it. The owner of the building, a lawyer, came down from the upstairs and said, "Sir, what are you doing? Are you nuts? Don't do this. Are you crazy?" I looked at him and said, "Morris, I'm doing this." There was this young mother who came in with a stroller and bought a slice of pizza. I stopped her and asked, "What do you think of the new sign?" She said, "I like it because it's not a chain anymore. It's a store within our community." That's an area where we can get the right feedback.

DP: Honest feedback. Starbucks was built on the Italian cafe premise. People want that cultural feeling. With our sign for instance, people thought that it looked more like a community store. It's not your typical place anymore. You know you're going to get a great product.

There's another milestone that we just reached: last year, the Canadian Franchise System voted us the number one franchise in franchise excellence out of 450 franchises. We're a local and regional chain, not a national one, but we still won that award. As a family operation, it hits home and it's great that we've achieved that award.

How much does being a family operation contribute to your success?

DP: It has a lot to do with it. We're not just looking at the dollars and cents. I mean, you have to be mindful of it to stay in business, but I think there's another intangible aspect to it. We operate the company as a family. Every year, we get together with our franchisees and their families. That creates a culture where people are interested because they have their own family businesses and shows that we're not just there to beat a person over the head. We are interested in our employees becoming successful and working with them. If they are successful, we become successful. We have employees that have been with us for thirty or forty years, which is unheard of today.

Where is the evolution of Italian food in Toronto headed?

SP: What has happened here is that Italian restaurants have copied American-Italian cuisine. Some of them have stayed the course. Terroni, for instance, stayed the course and makes simple, good food. Immigrants like me went back to Italy and saw that Italian food there is not what we call Italian food here. They use simple ingredients and then, only use two or three of them. Twenty years ago, you couldn't get a pizza cooked in a wood-fired oven. Now there are chains that cook pizza in a wood-fired oven and people have to have bufala mozzarella on their pizza, but in Italy, they use fior di latte. If you go to Mark McEwan's store fifty percent of the products he has are Italian. His stores aren't for the ordinary shopper but he is very influential. The evolution is that we have a well-known chef with North American cuisine experience deciding to go into the Italian market by opening up Fabbrica. He has rows of the best pasta that you can import from Italy. I have to give credit to some of the new restaurateurs. It's true that when Italians come here they think we are more Italian than they are.

I was in a restaurant in San Remo recently and the waiter asked where we were from. It turns out we lived about thirty minutes away from each other. He asked whether we ate lampascioni and a few minutes later showed up with a plate of them. It really struck me. I asked if he served them in the restaurant. He said, "Sam, you would not believe it. Here we are in San Remo, which is not in Southern Italy, but people are craving the old things now." What they are discovering now, we discovered maybe ten years ago in Canada: we've discovered that people want the old things.

DP: Italians have gone back to their comfort food. Going back and forth to Italy helps to bring ideas back and change the evolution. In Italy a lot of attention is paid to the ingredients and to the freshness of the ingredients. Here too you will see menus based on ingredients that are only in season. People love Italian food because it's tasty and it's simple and because they travel or because they live in a multicultural city. They are demanding it now. Chefs are bringing that to the table and changing our attitudes towards Italian cooking. It's all about the food and being in good company. Italians are not stuffy. They want a relaxed atmosphere. That is a characteristic of the successful restaurants today. Pizza Nova has a relaxed atmosphere but it's still bringing authentic taste.

And now you've added the focaccia barese.

DP: Yes, that's right. It's a recipe that comes from Bari from the consorzio. We have the IGP designation (Indicazione Geografica Protetta) in Canada to make that product. It's an authentic product. It has to be made that way. If we change it or add different toppings then it's not focaccia barese anymore.

What is the Pizza Nova philosophy and what will be its legacy?

DP: The philosophy is to produce a high-end quality product first and foremost. That has been our philosophy and legacy. For over fifty years people have gotten to know us because of our product and its quality.

SP: When you say Pizza Nova you want them to know that it's a high quality product and not just a pizza place.

DP: We want to continue to improve and bring in new things like the focaccia barese and the Italian sandwiches we brought in last year.

SP: We brought in the Italian hot peppers.

DP: Before the hot peppers were in a vinegar base. That's an American style pepper. We found peppers that are more authentic. That's what we're always looking to do. There's never a final step. We want people to be really loyal to us. When they see a new product they expect it to be the best because they're used to the best.

SP: We've added a Primucci line of products which features peeled tomatoes, hot peppers, and soon we'll be adding pasta sauce. The tomatoes in the pasta sauce are from Italy. We also have oil that is 100% Italian and certified organic.

When we first opened our store in 1963 there was this man named Mr. Fisher, a Volkswagen dealer who went up to his cottage every Friday night. Every Friday night he would call and order from us. One night he said, "I take your pizza up to my cottage and the cheese smudges." So to prevent this from happening I decided not to cut the pizza and to cook it a little bit less. Then I told him not to call anymore because Fridays at 5:00 p.m. there would be three slightly undercooked pizzas ready on the counter for him. He was our steady customer for 10 years and everybody knew him.

DP: Giving back to the community has also been very important. Back in the early 70s, they even did it. It's part of the DNA of the company. We need to give back because the community gives a lot to us as well.

SP: That started back in the day with Variety Village. There was a walk organized by Whipper Billy Watson and Harold Ballard. Ballard used to own the Toronto Maple Leafs and Whipper Billy Watson was a champion wrestler. They both loved to work with children.

DP: That's part of the legacy of Pizza Nova. We have a psychologist on staff, Mary, who worked here through her teens and her schooling. She started off at the Canadian National Exhibition store and then she worked in our call centre. We started to offer this service to our employees and franchisees: if anybody had an issue, they could talk to her at no charge. We wouldn't get involved. It's completely separate. It's done very well because not a lot of companies do that for their employees. Everybody has issues and it's good to have someone there to help you cope with them. It's a service to help them get better and it is part of our commitment to our people.

SP: And now there are whole families that come to see her. Some of the kids in the call centre even call her mom. The franchisees and the staff really appreciate it.

DP: It's a key component of who we are as a company. You can trace it back to the family business. You take care of your family and this is part of it.

SICILIAN ICE CREAM
712 College St. W.

Owners: Galipo family

Opened: 1959

Highlights: gelato, tartufo

Fact: Toronto's oldest gelateria. The Galipo brothers carried their grandfather's legacy of gelato making from Capo d'Olando, Sicily to College Street. The secret of this recipe? 100% fior di latte.

Quote: "Gelato runs through our veins."

Award: 2011 Top Choice Award for Top Gelateria

Photo: Denis De Klerck

PUSATERI'S

an interview with John Mastroianni

Tell me about Pusateri's beginnings.

JM: In 1957, Salvatore Pusateri immigrated to Canada from Sicily. Six years later, they decided to open up a small fruit store that quickly expanded into a meat market and later, into groceries. What they wanted to do was not only bring products from overseas to Canada, but to really bring the best of what was out there to Canada. They were originally on St. Clair West. That appreciation of quality passed on to his son, Cosimo Pusateri, who took over the family business in 1986.

Cosimo's vision was to grow the family business into a gourmet food emporium. Cosimo decided he wanted to evolve the business because he saw the market was changing in that area. He wanted to bring a wider selection of products than what people were used to when grocery shopping in an Italian market. Bringing it to the Avenue Road and Lawrence area was a challenge. Though it was difficult, eventually word of mouth really helped. The quality of the products coming in was nothing but the best: our philosophy was to get to the Food Terminal at three a.m. to get the best of what was available. Cosimo also saw a future in the business of prepared food. Back then, it was known as "Lean Cuisine" frozen dinners, but he wanted to offer consumers the kind of home cooked meals he had when he was a child. Back in the day, there was usually only one income earner so someone could be home to cook meals, but by 1986, there were dual income earners and people just didn't have time to cook anymore. He started up by opening a small kitchen in the back here. They were the typical Italian recipes that he was used to growing up.

Like an Italian gastronomia?

JM: Yes, but it was a very, very small kitchen. Of course, it has grown quite a bit: there is every kind of equipment you can think of back there. It started with everything from lasagna to couscous to potato salad. They were mostly dishes that took a really long time to prepare.

Was it a different public than now?

JM: It was a different public altogether. We were

catering to a much more multicultural clientele. It was very diverse. We started to see that they wanted more and more of the products we were preparing. We would roast red peppers in our parking lot and have twenty women cooking out there with barbecues. The peppers had to be done because it was peak season. People would come and watch to see how these artisanal dishes were created. It was like a show. We used locally-grown Ontario peppers. That's how we started many years ago before this current trend even started. We always promoted local. We dealt with a lot of private, local farmers who produced strictly for us. They only had 10,000 baskets of peaches and they would sell them only to us.

How did that affect what you could offer your customers in terms of fruit and vegetables?

JM: We started looking at greenhouses, for example. Then it became a bit of a challenge trying to satisfy the demands of the consumers. Many people wanted strawberries twelve months a year. We were bringing in strawberries from New Zealand in the winter because that was their summer. There was a cost, of course. Did they taste the same as our local strawberries? Absolutely not. The best produce is local and in abundance because it makes it less expensive. Forced ripeness is not ideal either. Sometimes, produce is picked when it has not yet ripened on the trees. We had to try to source every product under the sun all year long. Back in the 80s, there was no such thing as going on your computer and sourcing a product on Google. Our customers were well travelled. They would come back from Provence in France and ask for a particular olive oil. We would

have to find that olive oil producer via a person that we might know that lives in France or travels there often. It was extremely appreciated by consumers because they found someone that would take the time to develop the market and provide them with products right in their own backyard. Our lines quickly expanded and we kept on building and building. We brought in sun-dried tomatoes from Pachino because they had the best cherry tomatoes. We didn't want them oven-dried so they would ship them to us sun-dried. That was key for us.

Has technology heightened competition now that everything is accessible to everyone?

JM: It still comes down to your customers and your market. If you don't have the client base that will appreciate or understand the quality behind the products you are bringing in, there's no point. Nothing will sell. Our clients understand this. You need to understand who has the best products. Are you bringing in San Marzano tomatoes straight from Naples or are you buying the San Marzano seed that has been produced in California? It makes a difference. The microclimates are different. They don't have the same taste. There's a lot of passion behind products that are made all over the world. I mean, they're making things the same way that they've been made for centuries. You can try to mimic products but they'll still be second-rate. We have customers that really understand that.

Authenticity, in other words, is extremely important for Pusateri's.

JM: It's extremely important. It's critical that we maintain it. We want the next generation to understand and it's our job as retailers to educate the public. You can look at a kiwi and say it came from New Zealand, but Italians are producing kiwi which are outstanding as well. So there are different regions around the world making the same product, but are they truly the same product? Do they taste the same? Maybe sometimes they taste better. But certain products you just cannot compare.

Like Italian olive oil?

JM: Yes. The very first olive oil we introduced here was Italian. In 1989, we introduced Sassicaia olive oil. Most people are familiar with the wines they produce but they also make an olive oil. That was our first breakthrough into the specialty, gourmet market. We were selling a 750 ml bottle of olive oil for $29.99. You could have bought 3L tins of olive oil for $7.00 at the time. But we introduced this oil and people would taste it and fall in love with it. They understood it was not cooking oil but finishing oil. We don't recommend people spend a for-

tune on a bottle of olive oil for cooking. You want the product to complement what you're producing.

Was Pusateri's the first gourmet food shop?

JM: Cosimo was a pioneer and a visionary. I remember starting with him in 1988 and he took me with him on a weekend trip to New York. We went to visit some of the shops there: Balducci's, Dean and DeLuca, etc. What he saw there were good community shops but they lacked that global picture. They tried to concentrate on one ethnic group. Cosimo wanted to bring the best of what the world had to offer to Toronto. He wanted people to be able to find products here that they would be able to find back home, whether they were from Greece, Croatia, or Turkey.

At the same time, we saw that there was a need to educate our customers. We wanted them to understand the different meals they were eating at restaurants. We set out on a mission of bringing chefs and restaurant owners to our store to demonstrate how to properly cook ethnically diverse dishes with the ingredients we gave them. Sometimes, they would even provide us with things they had already cooked.

Who were some of these chefs?

JM: People like Massimo (Capra) from Mistura, Marisa (Rocca) from Sotto Sotto, Patrick (Kostiw) from the Four Seasons, and Keith (Froggett) from Scaramouche. There was really a range. They were pioneers in their own industries. It was very important for us to show our consumers that you could have that same restaurant meal if you had the right ingredients and you had the expertise in teaching. It helped build a great rapport with the consumers.

There was a dynamic.

JM: Definitely. While we were bringing in products, we also made an effort to bring in the people who were specialists in using and showcasing these products. They were passionate about talking about these products. It was a major turning point for us in our business too. We were extremely influential in creating a food network. This was a theatre before the Food Network existed on TV. People wanted to come and shop as an adventure. It wasn't a task. It was something people looked forward to. Times change and food is evolving. Today, people are more health conscious so we bring in nutritionists sometimes to talk to our consumers. I think, growing up, our generation kind of missed that part. Our prepared foods were a huge draw for customers. People saw that we didn't take shortcuts. We started aging beef in the same way that restaurants aged beef. For us it was always about getting the premium. We stuck with Canadian beef. Yes, we carried beef from the United States but that's because our customers

Photo: Deborah Verginella

travelled to the States and wanted to have the same product here. We were one of the first places to sell Kobe beef from Japan. They won't ship it anymore, but we had waiting lists of people who were buying it for $200.00 a pound. It was about the experience. People renovate their kitchens, entertain, and a lot of conversation centres around the food we eat.

I like to think that Cosimo's passing (in 1995) left a void in the industry because no one was thinking along the same lines he was. I felt honoured, he was a mentor to me. Food was his life and being able to bring it here made him proud. He felt the city deserved to be on the map. You don't realize it until you see the tourists come in here. Last year, we had a bus of tourists come. It was neat to see Pusateri's on their list of places to see in Toronto along with Casa Loma and the CN Tower. But it's important to also get people back into the food business. It's a struggle, but it's important. We need to attract people to come into the business and to stay in the business. It's exciting.

Are there plans for Pusateri's, surely one of the most iconic shops in this city, to expand beyond the city?

JM: The demand for our operation to expand into other markets with similar demographics to our own has grown. It would be very difficult to simply open up a dozen stores. Not every area in the city is an Avenue Road and Lawrence neighbourhood. You have to take baby steps to get into those markets. Our plan is to grow gradually in areas where we have the proper client base. Our plans are to grow because the demand is there from mayors in various cities in the United States or Canada. It's about people and availability of products.

In Toronto we're very lucky because the Food Terminal is tremendous. We can taste twenty different cantaloupes before we find the one that tastes the best. Does every other city have a Food Terminal like that? No. Logistics can become challenging. There is certainly room for us to grow in other areas in Canada and the United States. So expansion is a possibility.

Apart from the name, how does Pusateri's maintain its Italian character?

JM: Today, Italian is not what we knew of it twenty years ago. It's a staple. It's comfort. In the mindset of most people, it's become an international cuisine. The products that you use to make spaghetti and meatballs are international, mainstream products. Getting the right tomatoes and pasta to make it is still important. It's not about price because anybody can make spaghetti and meatballs, but how many people can make it the old-fashioned way? It's important for us to maintain that.

So Italian food has become a part of mainstream culture?

JM: Yes. It's mainstream in the same way that potato salad and macaroni and cheese, which are

Photo: Deborah Verginella

Photo: Deborah Verginella

Canadian, are mainstream. Our macaroni and cheese is made with fresh cheddar. We've even revolutionized that kind of a simple dish. You can travel through any small town in Italy and find a cultural dish that you will only find in that small town. That is great for us because it means that there is an endless list of products that we can introduce into this market. A simple thing like orecchiette is an example of this. For a long time, pasta was penne, rigatoni, spaghetti, and things like that. But now people can have this handmade product here and it's a delicacy. It's incredible. There's a lot that Italy has to offer.

What are the qualities that need to be present in a product for you to select it?

JM: The first thing I look for is the origin. Number two is the quality. Things have to be palatable for all consumers. I look at the representation that the company will have when marketing the product. I want them to be able to educate the consumer. The consumer needs to know why they should buy that product over somebody else's.

What is your most exciting project at the moment?

JM: There's always something happening over here! Our catering department has blossomed tremendously. There's a huge demand for consumers wanting our product on their kitchen table. We've seen that word of mouth has really helped this. They want us to be their chef and cook for them, like being guests at their own party. Our meat department is also great. Our meat manager, Joe, creates things that are incredible, like two-foot shish kabobs. It's something people will talk about at their tables. We also have our 'barbarian steak' which is a large piece of meat for someone to eat, but it's a spectacle to behold. Butcher shops are fading away but we really oppose this: we know what it takes to prepare a cut of beef and the importance of it. We are also aware of the challenges; I mean, how many people are training to be butchers in today's society? We need the younger generation to understand the profession. People still like to feel they have a butcher that's there. We don't have that luxury anymore.

We're also looking at having satellite operations to our catering industry. People can pick up their orders closer to their own homes rather than having to come into one of our full-blown stores. We're talking about mini Pusateri's. This is what we're thinking about when we think about our expansion. It's exciting to see how we are going to move forward to cater to these markets. It really is.

To us, the importance of having the history brought forward to our children and grandchildren is very valuable. It makes this job enjoyable.

VESUVIO PIZZERIA AND SPAGHETTI HOUSE

3014 Dundas St. W.

Owner: Pugliese Family

Opened: 1957

Menu highlights: New York-style pizza, pasta al forno

Fact: The oldest pizzeria in Toronto. The Pugliese family led the lobby against the "dry" designation of the Junction dating from 1903. It was not until the fifth attempt during the municipal election of 1997 that the designation of the Junction changed to "wet;" it won by one vote!

Photo Courtesy of Piera Pugliese

SOTTO SOTTO

an interview with Marisa Rocca

Can you give me a sense of this place, your story, your family, your food?

MR: Absolutely. This place began late in 1989 when I came to Canada. I spoke no English. I started out as a dishwasher in a little restaurant called Fieramosca, which is still around today. I did it just to grab any type of job. Why Toronto? I had a couple of friends here. Why did I come here and leave behind a beautiful city like Rome? Well, I didn't have much there. I can truly say I was pretty poor. We were struggling, so anything I was able to grab was good. My friend said, "Marisa, why don't you come to Toronto? It's a beautiful city. It's a young country. You're young enough to come to Canada and try. If it doesn't work, you can always go back." So that's what I did. When I came here, of course, it was hard for me. Without English, the only job I could get was as a dishwasher. I did very well. I was the best dishwasher in the city. The kitchen was very small there. I would wash dishes, do preparation, and do some cleaning with one of the cooks in the restaurant. How did I become a cook? One day he didn't show up for lunch and the restaurant got very busy. The waitress told me I had to cook. She said I had to because the restaurant was one quarter full. I had learned by watching. From that day on, I became the lunch cook because the people who ate there that day thought it was unbelievable.

What was the first dish you cooked?

MR: It was rigatoni cremonese which I sometimes still make. It's a dish with broccoli, cauliflower, and a tomato cream sauce. That's how I started to climb the ladder. I would cook lunch and dinner and also clean. My English was starting to get a little bit better—people liked that I could speak broken English. Sometimes, the words were really not proper at all, it almost made the food taste even better! It made the whole experience feel more authentic.

Fieramosca was a really authentic restaurant. I stayed there until I got married and opened up Sotto Sotto—so for a really long time. I got married in 1992 so twenty years ago. I'm going to have a party in the late fall to celebrate. There were five years in between. By the time I left Fieramosca I was a manager there. I understood then what starting a business really meant. And I developed a taste for food. When you're young you just want to get rid of where you come from. Then at the end, you bring everything back: you are your past. My memories of my town and my nonna making fresh pasta made me realize that that was my education. I didn't realize it at the time.

You came on your own?

MR: Yes, I came by myself. Then everyone else came. I didn't call them—they followed me!

There are a lot of pictures of your family here. They all became part of the story.

MR: Oh yes, absolutely. I came here by myself and I started Sotto Sotto by myself. For seven years I almost didn't see my husband because I was cooking, cleaning, going to the market, and doing everything. As my brothers arrived, they all became a part of this. The pioneer, the hard worker—that was me. Fabio took an ordinary wine list to the next level. Felice became an extremely good cook and then moved on with his own life. Everyone was really important in my life. When Fabio got married, mamma came and now she has become part of the fabric and identity of the restaurant.

Does she help out in the kitchen?

MR: Mamma makes the evening specials. The menu is what I created and it hasn't changed in twenty years. A lot of items are not on the menu but because I have the same staff in the kitchen, I can make them. If you ask me to make a lasagna you had here ten years ago, I may need a couple of days, but I can do it for you. I've removed myself from the kitchen but they can make everything even better than I do, nothing is pre-cooked.

Where are your chefs from?

MR: They are local. I have two main Italian chefs.

One, Matteo Renzi, has been with us for almost twenty years. I've maintained the structure of my restaurant. At Sotto Sotto it is really hard to eat a bad meal. I was talking to a friend yesterday and he said he could eat there forever. It's getting better and better. After eleven years, I said I wanted to have a family of my own so we had a couple of children. I stepped back a little, but I'm here. My brother is back looking after the wine. Mamma is here. During the day, the old-fashioned mamma is screaming at everybody. It's an institution. It cannot get better than this and it cannot get simpler than this. The simple ingredients make the difference to me.

Have you always sourced the ingredients from the same place?

MR: Yes. The tomatoes all come from Italy. A good tomato will not have much acidity, but it won't be too sweet, either. Sometimes we blend different types of tomatoes to get the best taste. I use extra-virgin olive oil, salt, pepper, and whatever herbs belong to a particular dish. That's very important to us. That's sometimes why we have long lineups here. It's important that we keep our ingredients pure. If I make a Piemontese dish, it's important that I do my research and use the proper ingredients before I present it to you and say this is from Piemonte. You cannot sabotage things.

Is there a lot of inspiration from the south on your menu?

MR: I try to balance things. Most of these dishes you would find in many Roman places. Some of it is mix and match. I mean, you can go to China and find an amatriciana but how do you make the amatriciana or the carbonara? I think it's important to define what's really Italian. It's like making a Ferrari and then another company copying it and calling it a Ferrari. The motor is not a Ferrari motor. When Toronto went through the Italian fusion revolution I had people coming to me and begging me not to change. I didn't. It was my choice. If it says on the menu pomodoro basilico, it is pomodoro basilico. It's nice and simple. Don't tell me I'm not Italian because I don't put meatballs on top of my pomodoro basilico! I'm very careful to stay true to who I am and where I come from. It's like the history of Rome or of Florence: you cannot change it. It's a structural thing.

How would you define your restaurant? There are different elements like the white linens, but it is also friendly and familiar.

MR: When you come to this restaurant you feel the owner who created it, there is history in this place. For me, the money was never important. For the longest time I would go home all excited to tell my husband that it was such a busy night and that everyone was really happy and had a great time. He would ask me how much money we made and I would say that I didn't know. To this day I won't be able to tell you how much I made last night. But if you ask me if everything was perfect last night and if the customers left with a smile, I can tell you. Sotto Sotto is an experience. Is it fine dining? Yes, it is. Sophia Loren has been in here a few times. But it has a strong sentimental feeling. It's Marisa and all the people that have worked with Marisa. It's what Marisa wants her customers to feel when they come here. It's part of my life.

There are so many pictures of celebrities who have eaten here. It's been a really successful place. With all the changes in the food scene here what do you do to remain competitive and maintain your character?

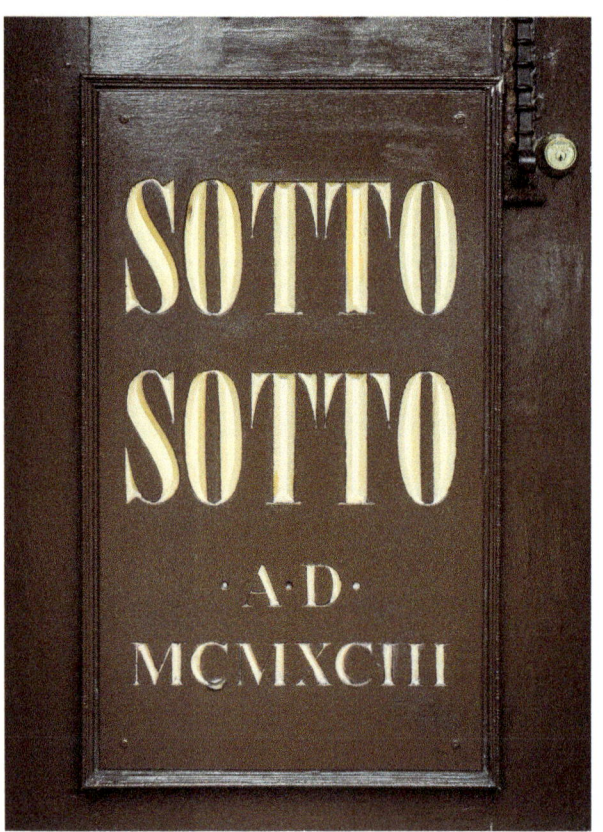

MR: Absolutely nothing. I've been doing the same thing for twenty years: traditional Italian cuisine. I can make you a simple plate of pasta with tomato sauce and burrata on the grill, and as a caterer, I can also create a very unique dish with an Italian flavour. I can do both. People keep coming and want the same dishes. They want me to open up in Los Angeles. It's about my simplicity at the end of the day, people come here and say they feel at home. Big names, executives and CEOs, and average people keep coming. After twenty years I get the same excitement when I come here. My best friend, Connie, is a night manager. Sometimes I sit with her and I say this restaurant is amazing and magical. I invite you to sit in the middle of the room to see what's really going on.

Is Italy still an inspiration for you? Do you go back often?

MR: Italy will always be in my heart even though I've become Canadian. Toronto gave me the opportunity to be who I am today and it does the same for many young people who try to immigrate to Canada. I would never have achieved in Rome what I achieved here. But for me, Rome is the source. It was my education. I try to go every year because it's very important. I talk to my kids in Italian and I want them to know about it and never forget it and pass it on to their children. Italy is like my fuel. I go there, I recharge, and then I come back. It has shaped what we try to bring to this country. There are new ideas emerging there, but at the end of the day, everyone always goes back to the old traditions.

Where is Italian food in this city headed?

MR: I think it's becoming a little more refined, even in the fast food sector. You can find Italian restaurants, but also a chain like Terroni. Terroni is not only a pizzeria, they deliver a beautiful sand-

wich or plate of pasta and yet, it's a casual place. That's the direction of the future. The younger generation likes Terroni and places that are less formal than they used to be. Nightclubs are sort of dying and young people, including me, want to have a pizzetta and sit at the bar and listen to great music. The layout of the restaurant is changing but I still believe that food has to be traditional and you have to provide good food in a new environment: places like La Bettola, where you can have a really nice sandwich with a good and expensive bottle of wine, or a little pizzeria, like Libretto. We need more places like that.

Today, people have knowledge, they travel, and they want more. They stay at wineries and do cooking classes. You can't fool them anymore. They know a lot. I love the fact that there are more and more pizzerias and casual places. I love seeing all of these new ideas. Italian restaurants have tended to prevail more than any other countries because Italian cuisine and Italian culture provides a little bit of everything. Look at what Italians have been able to accomplish in this country.

What has been your most memorable moment?

MR: My most memorable moment was when Sophia Loren walked in here for a private dinner one night. I had an emotional moment which I never thought I would have had in my life. I cried. The most beautiful thing was that she never ate at night and that night was just magical: she enjoyed the food. She complimented me on the food! For me, that was the most memorable night. She was my icon. When I lived in Italy you heard people say she was untouchable. It really made a difference in my life.

What is your signature dish? Your personal favourite?

MR: My personal favourite is the carbonara but I rarely have it. I also love the pasta all'amatriciana. Our signature dish is probably the grilled fish. It's to die for. The mamma lasagna that we make here is also to die for. Mamma doesn't put any cream in it and it's so simple. People just love it. It's tomato sauce, mozzarella, and a combination of meats that I can't divulge. It took me many years to train my people to make sure everything is fresh.

If you were to describe Italian hospitality with one word what would it be?

MR: Personality. My personality helped me become who I am today. The way Italians talk and describe things brings me back to my country. That's what Italy is all about. That defines who I am and what I try to transmit and give to my customers. This is what I bring with me.

VIA ALLEGRO
1750 The Queensway W.

Opened: 1998

Highlights: Golden Spoon Risotto: won first place in a prestigious competition of twenty chefs. Artisanal Vialone Nano riso simmered with slow cooked duck confit and agrodolce grape preserve, foie gras cream reduction, finished with balsamic vinegar of Modena.

Awards: The Supreme Whisky Award—Best Scotch List in the world from *Whisky Magazine* of London, England. The Grand Award, the most coveted and esteemed wine award in the world from *Wine Spectator Magazine*.

Philosophy: "Once you are out of Italy, it is not authentic anymore. Let it be original! It is better to be original than trying to be authentic outside of Italy."

Photo Courtesy of Via Allegro

TERRONI

an interview with Cosimo Mammoliti

Tell me a little about you and your relationship with Italy.

CM: I was born in Canada. My parents are both from Calabria. My relationship with Italy started around the age of seventeen because that was the first time I went to Italy. I fell in love with the culture, and the food, and everything. When I came back to Canada, I knew that I just had to get back to Italy. At that point, I was just finishing school and then I started working in the restaurant business at seventeen. I did dishwashing, salad prep, food running, and worked in bars.

Did you work in an Italian restaurant?

CM: Yeah, it was an Italian restaurant called Noodles and it was run by Dante Rota and his family. I'm still really good friends with Carlo (his son). It was located at Bay and Bloor. That was my first real restaurant job. It was in 1985, I think. I started off there and then I worked in different restaurants: Orso, all of the important ones. I knew that I wanted to work in the restaurant business and that I was pretty much done with school. I loved Italian culture. I started the restaurant in 1992. It was more of a shop and not a restaurant in the beginning. I ran it with a friend who was importing foods from Italy. I was more concerned with the restaurant side of things. But it was more of a shop because we didn't have a lot of money to open up a restaurant. We started off on Queen Street because the rent was cheap.

That was the first location?

CM: That was the first location. It had four stools. We were selling espresso, we were making panini. It was a local, little deli. It was a place people could come and get their coffee in the morning. It really took off from there.

What was Queen Street West like then?

CM: It was not pretty. It was a rough area. In 1992 there was nothing there. There were prostitutes outside. There was a bar across the street that was well-known, but it was at the end of its run.

So how did a new place survive in an area like that?

CM: We were two young kids and we didn't really have a lot of money. The rent was cheap and we just took a chance. If we had known any better we definitely wouldn't have gone to that area. We jumped on the fact that we had an opportunity to do something.

You introduced a new concept to the city with Terroni. You made the concept of osteria/pizzeria familiar to a Canadian audience. How did you know the time was right and that people would be receptive to it?

CM: I wasn't a genius. Everything was done basically on experience and feeling and passion and from what I had learned on my trips to Italy. My wife is Italian. She was born in Milano and grew up in Bari. I met my wife before I opened and my roots got stronger. I spent a lot of time in Puglia so a lot of what I put out at my restaurant was influenced by that. I spent more time in Puglia than I did in Calabria. We started off importing olives, olive oil, taralli, orecchiette, and other traditional stuff from Puglia. From making sandwiches, we would put out insalate and then a pasta al forno because those were easy things to make without a full kitchen. After about a year, once we started making some money, we put in a pizza oven. We went at a really slow pace. And then we started adding more typical pugliese dishes that I had experienced from my travels in Italy. As Terroni on Queen Street grew, we reinvested all of the money and brought in a full kitchen. We went from four stools to thirty stools and later to fifty stools. And the menu just evolved. It was very natural. It was not planned. We did what we could. As soon as we could add another piece to the puzzle because we could afford to, we would. Once the menu and the food started taking its own course, we got involved in the wines. We started bringing our own flour to make the pizza as well as our own tomatoes. All of the olive oil and taralli come from Puglia. The tomatoes come from Campania. The flour comes from le Marche. The water comes from Bologna. About seven years ago we started bringing in the wines. Our company is called Cavinona and again, we started off really small and then it just evolved. What I have a lot of fun with is improving the quality of the food and the quality of the products. That's what I know I have complete control over.

That's what allowed you to open all of the locations?

CM: Actually, no. All of the locations got me to that point. Victoria Street opened about three years later and up here at Balmoral we opened in 2000. After that, I can't even keep track of what happened. We opened in Los Angeles, and then there was L'Osteria and La Bettola.

Let's talk about La Bettola: how did you make the decision to expand from Terroni to a sort of chain of restaurants?

CM: Terroni was on Queen Street, Victoria Street (which moved to Adelaide), then here on Balmoral, and Los Angeles. Terroni is a strong name, it's great, and the menu has remained more or less unchanged. When I moved Terroni to Adelaide, I kept the space empty for a year. At that point, I couldn't put another Terroni there so I decided to do something else. L'Osteria opened up first in the old Terroni location. I really wanted to do something different. The idea was to bring the experience of what I ate in Puglia to Toronto. I wanted people to get into that mentality. It was totally a love kind of thing. It was more to do something for fun. I knew the price point was too much, but all of the pasta was made by hand and not machines. To this day, I just don't think people ever got into the mentality of the osteria. The city is more of a pizza and pasta kind of place. L'Osteria has a great menu and what you get is great value for quality and the food is at a different level. It definitely had its own clientele. Some customers from Terroni will come, but not all of them. That's why La Bettola opened up. Then the space next door opened up.

The La Bettola experience is similar to Terroni?

CM: Yes. The idea was to offer a simplified Terroni menu. It's a miniature version of Terroni. The Terroni menu is so big. It worked out and it was down the street from Terroni. There are three restaurants basically on the same street.

Do you think people here find that dining experience more appealing?

CM: I think it is the perfect mix of the two. It offers a balance of everything. We're definitely a pizza and pasta place for sure, but there are some great secondi as well.

Is it because it provides North Americans with what they need—a fast experience instead of a slower Italian experience?

CM: I have to think that's the case. At lunch time, people don't have the time. You can eat fast at L'Osteria, but it is still slowed down. We wanted people to experience that. It was our whole idea. It was never about the price point because it was inexpensive. It's probably less expensive than Terroni, but people just want to dine faster.

What else besides the leisurely pace is it about L'Osteria that makes it a little more sophisticated?

CM: I think it's more traditional. It's more authentic.

We'll do a ribollito night on Monday nights. On Saturdays we do a meat night wwith coniglio. It's a diverse menu for sure.

How do you think you've contributed to more than just feeding people Italian food?

CM: I'm not really sure that most people know exactly what we do. People come and they like what they eat and there's a good vibe. I'll sit down and explain to people how we source all of the products we use. You know, the water and the coffee come from Italy because we think it's what works the best. I'll tell people the eggs we use to make the pasta come from Manitoba and they always ask why. It's because the eggs used to make pasta in Italy are yellow and give the pasta a nice colour. We tried to find those eggs for years here. I think that people come back and that's great. By doing the things that we do, I hope that's the reason why. I bring in wines that no one else will bother trying to bring in from Etna or Valle d'Aosta. They're often more difficult to sell, but the beauty of the restaurant getting bigger is that I can control completely what I put on the table. I don't bring it in for benefits. I don't bring it in to rack up the prices. I do it because it's my job. What most people think of Italy is not what Italy really is. There's a lot more to it than most people think.

You famously don't allow ingredients to be substituted in your dishes; how do you do this and still please the client?

CM: That's probably the hardest part. When you read complaints from people they're mostly about the 'no substitutions' rule. They can't get their pizza cut, they can't mix the balsamic vinegar in with the oil, or they can't get parmigiano for the pasta. Most people think that the customer is always right and should get what they want. I value all of my customers and want them to be happy, but if I allow people to make substitutions I won't be staying true to my heart and who I am. My whole process is to try to do things as traditionally as possible. Some people don't accept or understand that. We've been adamant since day one that we don't change things. In Italy people know food. If they ask for a substitution it's going to be one that makes sense. They'll ask for a margherita with olives, for example, and that makes sense: I'll do that. But then the person beside you is going to ask for a margherita with smoked salmon on it and that doesn't make sense. If I change it for one person, then I have to change it for everybody.

Putting aside the fact that you are Italian, what do you think it is about Italian food and culture that makes it universally appealing?

CM: For me personally, I think the beauty of Italian food is its simplicity. It has nothing to hide. It's about the products. My menu is very simple and that's what makes it different from a place down the street. I source the best product. In the summer I go to Italy with my kids. We'll go to the beach at Lido and they'll have a fresh, grilled fish that goes right into a panino. I could never do that here because the fish isn't coming fresh from the sea. But Italian food is simple and a lot of people try to complicate it and screw it up. People like Italian cuisine because they can eat it every day as well as multiple times a day. You don't feel bloated. It's not heavy. When you leave you feel good. I've gone to so many restaurants where the food is heavy and rich and I can't digest it.

Your menu is pretty straightforward. Do you have a fixed menu or does it change with the season?

CM: We change it once a year. We do a summer menu and a winter menu. The summer menu is lighter. The thing that changes most is probably the pasta. In the winter we make heavier pastas with ragù.

What is the story behind the name, Terroni?

CM: Back when we opened up we were two young guys: we were going to call it I Due Terroni because he was from Bari and I was from Calabria. We were talking to one guy on the street who had an iconic antique shop on Queen Street. We told him the name and he said that we needed to make it simpler because it was too long and that we needed to think of a stronger name. We were young and we didn't think about it much, so we called it Terroni. To us, it seemed like a fun name. We weren't trying to make fun of it or anything. All I knew was that my parents were called terroni and it wasn't a great thing to be called that. But we were proud to be from the south and proud of our heritage, so we found it very fitting to open up a little shop called Terroni and to see what happened.

I think for many people, Terroni is the place to go if you want a thin-crust pizza. What is it that makes your pizza so good? What's the secret?

CM: I don't have a crazy secret. Again, I think it has to do with the flour we use. We now have our own flour that's milled for us in le Marche from a master baker who has been working with us because we're opening up a bakery on Queen Street.

An Italian bakery?

CM: Yes. I am so excited about the bakery. It's going to be so great. It's all natural. The head baker, Fabio, worked under this baker in Italy, Giuliano, for a number of years. He's the nicest young guy. He's making all of the breads and we're also going to be making homemade pizza al taglio. I have this other young guy, Armando, who is from Napoli and he will do some desserts. He just joined the team. It's going to be so authentic.

Where on Queen Street?

CM: It's two doors east of Terroni. All the bread is traditionally made. I'm so obsessed with it because I always knew a little bit about bread and have always wanted to make it, but again, the bakery is a necessity. I just got tired of waiting for bread to be delivered late to the restaurants. One day the bread was good and the next day it wasn't. Since we have six or seven restaurants it made sense to open a bakery just for me. I did the same thing with the wines. We don't sell to anyone else. They're just for us. That's the best part. We can totally control everything. But back to the pizza, again, I think it just has to do with the flour and the ingredients that we use.

You talked earlier about Terroni in Los Angeles. How did that happen?

CM: A girl who used to work for me moved to Los Angeles and got into her own businesses with clubs and restaurants. We kept in touch and always said we should open up a Terroni there. She went on and did her own thing and I was doing my thing, and about six years ago, the time was right and I visited her in Los Angeles for the first time. As soon as I got back to Toronto after being there for a couple of days she called me and said that she found a space and that I needed to go back. I went back and it just happened. I went into partnership with her. My best friend Max, who is from Bologna, was working with me here but needed to expand because he was very talented. The opportunity was perfect for him, so he moved to Los Angeles. He's running it and it's doing well. We're opening up a second location there. We should be ready to open by the end of May, I hope. The second location will be more like the Adelaide Street location.

What made Terroni successful in that market? It's a big city and I imagine the competition must be quite tough.

CM: You know what? Los Angeles is a big city and there are a lot of restaurants, but we opened up quietly in a neighbourhood and it took off. I'm not really sure why. We were very fortunate. I think the fact that there are a lot of Canadians down there might help. We started off in a neighbourhood similar to Queen Street, but it's good to see that people have taken to it. It's been five years since we opened.

Your favourite dish?

CM: My favourite antipasto dish is definitely the funghi assoluti. That's a dish I actually came up with so I'm biased, but it is my favourite.

Did you work in the kitchen?

CM: Originally I did. I used to make pizza. The orecchiette are my favourite pasta. I love the Santo Spirito pizza. I'm very traditional.

And when you travel to Italy for vacation you go to Puglia?

CM: Yes. In the summertime, my wife goes to Italy because her family is all there. We have four children and they need to see their grandparents.

UNICO AND PRIMO FOODS

an interview with John Porco

Can you highlight some of Unico's history?

JP: Unico has a long history in Canada. It was the first Italian food company to have been established in Canada. It evolved from a small grocery store in downtown Toronto on King Street in 1917 into a distributor during the 1950s and 1960s. It began to distribute nationwide and in 1967 we moved into our current location in Vaughan. That's our head office.

Unico has gone through several ownership changes over the years. It has existed for almost one hundred years. The Iacobelli family is the current owner of Unico. They own Sun-Brite Foods and acquired Unico in 1997. John and Henry Iacobelli are out of Leamington, Ontario and acquired Unico for strategic reasons. Prior to their acquisition we have had many owners. Some, like the investment companies, did not have a long-term vision. Because of the new ownership I think we're in the right hands regarding our type of foods. We're in the Mediterranean food business. You need to understand food and food quality. Now that we're in private hands we've really grown our business dramatically. I've been with the company since 1981. I'm the Chief Operating Officer and run the day-to-day operations and report to the ownership. We've been able to look at our business and understand what was required to grow it on a national basis. What we've done is focus on quality, expand our product line, and work on our marketing. Of course our origins are in Ontario but you can find Unico products from coast to coast. We do business with big retailers like Sobey's, Loblaw, and Metro, but also with small retailers and grocery stores in Toronto and throughout Canada. Our products are very well-aligned and have a great tradition.

My background is in the food business. My dad owned a small grocery store on the east side of Toronto on Gerrard Street. It opened in 1960 and we had a Unico sign. People remember that. When we opened the store, I was two-years-old and would stay in the store a lot. We would hear that people arriving from Italy were told to look for the stores with the Unico sign; you could find good, Italian products there. Immigrants would come in right off the boat from Italy to our store in Canada. My dad would ask them how they had heard about the store and they would say they were told to look for the

signs. The signage project was a brilliant marketing strategy on the part of the company. People call me to this day and ask for signs, but we don't do that anymore.

From there, we got into what we call Mediterranean foods. We appeal to all ethnic backgrounds. Obviously we keep our Italian origins, but we are looking for ways to really grow the business. We have people coming from all parts of Europe and they have similar traditions so our product line is really well-positioned. We're talking about tomatoes that we plant and pack at our facility in Leamington, the olive oil packaged in Toronto, and olives coming from Europe. We've got the most extensive product line. Our current ownership is thinking about how to add more value and more quality. It's all about passion. When you're a big multinational you may lose some of that, but we're always thinking about how to produce the best Italian and Mediterranean products for the community. We're not going to make peanut butter. So that's really our story. We have sales people around the country and we're in every major retailer across the country. We're the largest company in Canada of this type.

Tell me a little about Primo.

JP: Primo was acquired in 2006 from an investment consortium. Prior to that it was owned by Kraft. When we acquired it there were a lot of opportunities for Primo, Unico, and our parent company Sun-Brite, because of the product line they carried. But there wasn't a lot of attention paid to Primo. It was a brand that started up in 1956 in Toronto. It started off as pasta but it had a lot of other products too. It was privately held and then sold to many multinationals. It went through many ownership changes. Within ten years, the company had five owners. The last owner was Kraft. We approached them and thought we could do more with the business than they could. We got into exclusive negotiations with them and took over the company in August 2006.

We had to spend a lot of money updating the business. We have a large pasta-making facility right in the middle of Toronto at Highway 400 and Highway 401. When it was built in 1956 it was on the outskirts of the city. Now it's right in the middle and it's interesting because you wouldn't think of building a large pasta plant in the middle of the city. We've had a lot of capital investments in that plant since we took over. We've installed new high-tech pasta machines from Italy and we just completed another installation of a short goods pasta machine. These are the best pasta machines in the world. We did a lot of research. They are highly efficient, require little manual intervention, and create a quality product that is second to none, comparable to the best pasta in the world. The Primo business has an important heritage and has a lot of great growth opportunities all across the country. It's also distributed at all the major retailers. We're in good, wholesome nutritious foods. We've done a lot of marketing on behalf of both brands. When we were owned by an investment company, they didn't care too much about being involved in the community. I initiated that with the new ownership. We sponsor a lot of the ethnic media in Toronto and special Italian events like the CHIN Picnic. We're a big part of the community even though we're a big, national company. We appreciate the support we get. These two brands have been described as brands people grew up with. They may have lost their way for a while, but now they've come back. They're iconic brands in the Canadian marketplace. There are small brands that are very regionalized in Toronto or Quebec for example, but nobody goes national like Unico and Primo. We owe a lot to our heritage and to the ownership. I owe a lot to growing up in the business and understanding the difference in the quality between products. It's in my DNA. Since I was a little kid, it was my dream to work for Unico. Now, not only do I work for it, but I manage the day-to-day operations. It's not a job. It's a lifestyle. You're doing everything you can to make the business successful.

How has the culture of Italian food evolved in this city?

JP: The growth of, and the feeling for Italian food, have been phenomenal. People love food and are attuned to what's happening more than they were maybe twenty years ago. Having channels like the Food Network and reading cooking magazines have helped. Decades ago people didn't understand the difference between regular olive oil and extra-virgin olive oil. Today, everybody wants extra-virgin. People didn't understand balsamic vinegar. We're now the largest importer of balsamic vinegar in the country. People are learning. Now we even have a

balsamic glaze which is the next step up. It's becoming more than spaghetti and meatballs. That's what Italian food was about in the 1960s, but now it's about quality. Italian food is the most loved food in the world.

How much have Unico and Primo as brands contributed to this evolution?

JP: I think they've played a large part. I've been travelling around the country for about thirty-two years now. When I go to Regina, Saskatchewan, or somewhere in Newfoundland, people are eager to learn more, but they don't know a whole lot. They look at our companies as being the leading companies and want to be educated on the culture of Italian eating.

When we talk to them about getting our products into their customers' hands because that's what they want, retailers want to try that. The hub of the ethnic community in Toronto understands these products, but when you take them to different areas of the country, they're not as well known, but growing in popularity.

You've said that some products are imported from Europe and some are produced locally. How challenging is it to manufacture an Italian product on Canadian soil?

JP: Because of our long-standing tradition and how we've evolved over the years, we're able to do some things very well in this country. We've invested in the machinery and the technology.

For example, our pasta machines at Primo: They're the best pasta machines in the world and by using high quality Canadian wheat, we are able to produce a product that is very comparable to the best pasta in Italy. We've got the Italian technology, the local quality products, and we're very comparable. It's the same with our tomatoes. Our tomatoes are grown in southwestern Ontario around Leamington, the tomato capital of Canada. We select the farmers who harvest the tomatoes and we select the way we process them. If you taste an Ontario-grown tomato in the summertime, there is nothing like it. The Italian-grown tomatoes are just as good. A lot of our machinery, as well as the processing of our tomatoes, is Italian. We've brought a lot of Italian technology and Italian machinery into Canada and we've been able to produce the products here. Obviously there are some products that cannot be produced here, like olive oil. There are no olives here for commercial purposes. So that's produced and packaged for us in Italy. Olives in general, peperoncini, balsamic

vinegar ... these are things we have to import from the best suppliers in Italy. I think we're good corporate citizens. We support the local economies in the places we work. We have hundreds of people that work for us in our three businesses, we invest in Canada, but we also look for the best quality. If the best quality isn't here, we import it. In many cases, things come from Italy. We have a great relationship with our Italian suppliers.

What would you say is the essence of Italian products?

JP: It's all about flavour and passion. Italian food brings out a lot of passion in people. They love to talk about olive oil, they love to talk about pasta, they love to talk about tomatoes and olives. When people think about Italian food, they think about family, being with friends, and entertaining. There's a romance with Italian food that isn't there with a lot of other foods. We're trying to bring that feeling to consumers all across the country.

How do you know when people are ready to embrace a new product?

JP: We do our research. We do focus groups. Some of it is gut feeling. We travel around the world and find out what's trending. It's a long process. It's hard to introduce a new product but we do a lot of homework to get to know the potential of a product. Once we determine the potential of something we can source it cost-effectively and come up with a brand strategy. Everything isn't always successful, but we do a lot of work beforehand.

What is the most successful product you've launched?

JP: That's a tough question. Unico has approximately 400 products. Primo has more or less the same number. To single out one particular product is difficult because when I make an Italian meal, I don't use only one product, I use multiple products.

Photo: Deborah Verginella

So we put the same amount of effort into each one. I love our beans, but I also love our pastas and olive oils. It's impossible for me to pick one.

What are the advantages of being an Italian food manufacturer in Canada?

JP: We were the original Italian food distributor. We have a lot of history and a lot of knowledge. Because of our heritage people grew up with our brands, but this doesn't mean we can just sit back and twiddle our thumbs. We still need to look for ways to improve. We're driven by that. It's never-ending. We have an advantage because we've been around for a long time, but we manage the business like a small company.

In terms of pasta, is the pasta imported from Italy your greatest competition?

JP: Pasta is pasta is pasta. Some companies manufacture the pasta at plants in the United States but then have an Italian label, so what's the difference between that and what we make? We do look at the Italians, but we look at domestic competitors as well. The one thing we've done is improve the quality dramatically. We have our own mill which no one else in the country has. We have the machines I spoke about earlier. We want to produce pasta comparable to the pasta that comes out of Italy and we've done that. People may think otherwise, but I can assure you the technology we've invested in and the quality of wheat we can source means our quality is second to none.

What is your favourite dish?

JP: I love pasta. My wife loves to make me pasta. I can have it in any way, shape, or form. Henry Iacobelli, the owner and president, is very meticulous about quality. He's in the latter stages of his career and wants to buy only our products so he's always telling us to make sure we're manufacturing a high quality product.

ZAZA ESPRESSO BAR

75 Yorkville Ave., 775 St Clair Ave W.,
140 La Rose Ave., 256 Beresford Ave.

Owner: Raffaele Betallico

Opened: 2003

Highlight: espresso and cappuccino made from
Zaza coffee beans imported from Italy

Fact: The name is inspired by the cheeky post-war Neapolitan song Dove stà Zazà?, which tells the tale of Zazà, a flighty woman who leaves her Neapolitan lover to go after an American soldier. Every customer is greeted by either a "Ciao Bella" or "Ciao Bello," which rises above the Italian music that blasts in this tiny, chaotic bar.

Quote: "Drink Zaza's coffee every day and you'll be
happy like me your whole life long!"

ZUCCA

an interview with Andrew Milne-Allan

What's your first memory of food?

AMA: My first memory of food ... well, I have a whole bunch of memories from those early years. Beef dripping on toast with a little salt on top. That was my snack when I came home from school.

Did your mom make that?

AMA: Yes. My mom was a great cook. She was a simple cook, but she made everything with love and care. My dad tended really well to our vegetable garden. I can still recall the smell of those vegetables. I loved the smell of Swiss chard when it is being boiled.

So you loved all of those things even as a child?

AMA: Oh yes. Absolutely. We had a seasonal garden, but in New Zealand the seasons are long.

Did your mom cook traditional English food?

AMA: Well, my background is Scottish, but the New Zealand cooking was based on traditional English food. We ate a lot of vegetables and roasts. My father's palate was fairly conservative. Sometimes she would make spaghetti and my father would cut it up with a knife and fork.

Tell me about your passage from that to now, cooking Italian food.

AMA: I absorbed my mom's cooking without really cooking or helping out. I moved away from home when I was quite young. I was seventeen or eighteen-years-old. I always cooked for myself and I enjoyed it. I got quite fond of it and then I started cooking in restaurants to put myself through school.

This is still in New Zealand?

AMA: Yes. By chance, I worked in really good restaurants. At one of these places I was the dishwasher, but the dishwasher was located really close to the kitchen so I ended up being quite involved.

What were you studying?

AMA: I was doing an Arts degree and a Fine Arts degree. I was in school trying to figure out what I wanted to do. I was having dinner parties with my friends. I was also an artist and a so-called photographer. When I came to Canada, that's how I thought I would make a living. Reality bit fairly quickly. I saw a sign that said "Cook Wanted" and I applied. It was one of those sharp left turns that you make in your life. It was on Queen Street—the Beggar's Banquet.

What kind of food did you cook there?

AMA: It was vegetarian and David Cohlmeyer ran it. He now has Cookstown Greens. He was a hippy American draft dodger whose concept of a restaurant was very in vogue at the time. He thought everyone should eat at communal tables and there should be a new menu every night. If it was Tuesday, it was Belgian night, and if it was Friday, it was Swiss night. It was a very crazy concept.

What year was that?

AMA: 1974 or 1975. It was shortly after I arrived. The concept was okay. When I started, he wanted me to research dishes. I spent a lot of time in libraries studying and coming up with Moroccan dishes or Greek dishes or whatever.

So how did it become Italian for you?

AMA: Well, Italy was one of the rotating days. My partner Greg, who was also cooking there, and I, decided to buy the place. People told us it was a great idea and we loved food so we should do it. We decided that it made more sense to have each country feature for one week and not for one day. Over time, of course, this focus became narrower to more Mediterranean cuisine.

This was Peter Pan?

AMA: No, the Parrot. Peter Pan was down the street. It was a Chinese greasy spoon. We were the first one on that street. Peter Pan came after us. We bought the place in 1976. I was the chef. Greg (Couillard) still cooked, but he managed the front of the restaurant. He would come in and I would tell him, "Let's make this soup today." I would coach him through the recipe. Over time, Italian became my favourite thing to cook. We closed the restaurant the first May after we opened and took a trip to Italy.

What was that experience like?

AMA: It was mind-blowing. I remember the simple pasta dishes with just the day's catch and it was so fresh and amazing. It wasn't tourist season, so we were these two oddballs in this small town in Liguria.

After that trip, did Italy become the focus?

AMA: I kept the rotation. It became tighter as time went on. We did France, Morocco, Italy, and Greece. We introduced fish. We got a liquor license. It became more about the consumer experience. It wasn't really until I sold the Parrot, in and around the time that I met Gianna, my wife, that I really decided I wanted to cook Italian. We travelled to Italy and to New Zealand. Then I got involved with Giancarlo's. I feel very natural cooking Italian food. It never felt like I was cooking something foreign. It came very naturally to me.

What was the scene like at the time? Which restaurants were around?

AMA: There were places like Vittorio's up on Yonge Street. That was 'fifteen different ways to eat veal,' which was very typical of the time. La Scala was still going. There weren't too many places that were doing what I was doing.

What about sourcing your ingredients? What was the supplier landscape like at that time?

AMA: Well, I always visited markets. I would ride my bike to Kensington Market. I do the same thing now, just with a car and not a bicycle. Bertozzi and Aurora were suppliers that I dealt with, so they were up and running. There was no explosion of extra-virgin olive oil like we have now. We used olive oil and we were happy to have it. Nobody knew about extra-virgin olive oil in those days.

There were a few young entrepreneurs at the time who were bringing in things like balsamic vinegar. I was learning as I went along though. They were early days. It's not the way it is now. They would bring in interesting amari. Wine agencies were also starting out so we could expand the wine list and the liquor list.

What is it about Italian food that makes it so universally appealing?

AMA: Italian food is very approachable and easily understood. It's not an intellectual cuisine. It's a warm weather cuisine so people feel happy when they eat it. I think the accessibility and simplicity of Italian cuisine are great. It has bright colours and tends to be healthy. What is there not to like? It is probably the most popular cuisine in the world.

Talk to me about your progress going on to Bar Italia and now, Zucca?

AMA: Bar Italia was an interesting project. I was friends with Eugene, the owner. I had a lot of friends that wanted to open restaurants but didn't know how to go about putting together a menu. I

tried to channel his Calabrese roots. It was going to be his place and not mine. It made it easy for me to work on dishes that would work in that environment. It was 'elbows on the table' type food.

That is an iconic menu. How does that feel?

AMA: Well, it's great. I hear people tell me that the food is not the same and sometimes I will walk by and think that's not what I did.

It may not be the same, but it still must feel incredible to know that your menu has lasted that long.

AMA: It does for sure. We didn't realize it at the time, but it was quite unique and original.

I still miss the baccalà e freselle!

AMA: Me too. I've revisited that dish many times with Zucca. I remember Jamie Kennedy telling me it was his favourite dish. It feels great for me. It does.

Moving into Giancarlo's made me interested in more regional Italian food. I tried to explore and do the best I could at understanding the idea behind the dish.

What about Zucca and your philosophy there?

AMA: I suppose that really it's been a straight progression from the days when I first caught the Italian cuisine bug. I still like to respect tradition and the regional traditions. I do still like to put my twist on things. Maybe my palate has become more complex over time. I have a greater repertoire now of tastes and ingredients and ideas. I'm more confident. I improvise. I'm not stuck in one particular way of looking at things. There are dishes that I might make that you wouldn't find in Italy, but have an Italian spirit.

Give me an example.

AMA: Well, today we're making a stuffing for casoncelli, which is a stuffed pasta dish from Northern Italy, in Lombardia. It's an interesting dish because the stuffing always has multiple ingredients: fruit, nuts, meats, etc. It's an amalgam of things. There are two or three traditional versions. I've absorbed the message and am doing things a little differently. This still suits the palate. There's Savoy cabbage, cinnamon, raisins, and a variety of different meats. We'll serve that tonight with a leek sauce and sage. It's a riff on a traditional idea. The pasta is made in the traditional way still. I'm keeping that framework but am working with what I have and what's in season. I'm not Italian. I have the luxury of being able to visit all regions.

Did that surprise people when you started?

AMA: Yes. It comes out less now. There are more Italians that come to Zucca now because they know that we're one of the better Italian restaurants. They've gotten over that. Initially, it was not the case. We were always a little bit under the radar.

Tell me about locating Zucca in midtown.

AMA: It's good because the homes up there in Rosedale and Forest Hill are inhabited by wealthy people. That stretch of Yonge Street is a bit dead; it wasn't very auspicious. A lot of the people that came down to Giancarlo's came from there so I thought I would go closer to them. I commute now. It's not a neighbourhood that I feel all that comfortable in. It's a great area for business, but I wouldn't want to live there. We have people that have come forever and now their kids are coming for baptisms and confirmations. It's great. You always have to keep challenging yourself. I can only keep doing this if I'm trying new dishes.

Where does your inspiration come from?

AMA: It comes from the produce that comes each season. Farmer's markets are huge inspirations but they have only been around for the past ten years. I read a lot and I think a lot.

What do you read?

AMA: I read cookbooks to get inspiration for cooking, but I also read a lot of literature.

Is there anyone in particular you like? Do you like Ottolenghi?

AMA: I've read a little bit of Ottolenghi. The English have a lot of great cookbooks. They're very attached to Italian food. When Nigella is doing an Italian cookbook you know it's a serious trend! Or Carluccio. I watch a lot of his TV shows.

Is there a product that is now widely available that has changed the way you cook?

AMA: I think extra-virgin olive oil is one of them. It has changed my cooking in the sense that for the last decade or more we've been using extra-virgin olive oil as a raw condiment. Before we used to use it as just something to cook with. It lightens the food. It has really changed how I cook at Zucca. We use different oils for cooking, for dressings, and for raw condiments.

What do you see as the future of Italian food in this city?

AMA: I still feel that we're a little bit out on our own as far as appreciating what Italian food is really about. Terroni has done a great job, I think. They're mass-market but they've done a great job of making people aware of regional food. It's mostly specific

to the Puglia and Calabria regions. Too many Italian restaurants are happy to be generic. They rely on the unsophistication of their clientele to push their idea of what Italian food is.

So Torontonians can handle more?

AMA: Oh absolutely. In other cities it might be a little better. I'm going to San Francisco in the summer and I'm really looking forward to it because I've heard their regional Italian cuisine is very highly regarded. Toronto is a little behind in this respect. There aren't very many restaurants where you think, "that is Trevisano" or "that is Calabrese." I enjoy all of the regional cuisines. I like to know the backstory.

Do you have a favourite region?

AMA: I think Sicily. I love all of the southern cuisines, but I think Sicilian is a little bit more complex than the others. It's a sun cuisine. I just love the warm weather.

When you close your eyes and think of Italy, what is the dish in front of you?

AMA: Well, I would be on a patio facing the sea. There would be a breeze and it would be hot. It would definitely be seafood. Pasta con le sarde would be nice. Pasta with calamari or any kind of crudo with raw fish would be something I would love. Five years ago we were in Sicily. It was great. I would love to go back.

When you go back to Italy is there anything that surprises you food-wise?

AMA: They're following more the European and the North American model. They're losing sight of the basic principles of their cuisine.

Isn't that just a general global trend?

AMA: Yes. Globalization has a lot to do with it, for sure.

Do you think it ties in with the chef-as-celebrity trend?

AMA: Yes, it has a huge impact on it. There's the competition for Michelin stars and stuff like that.

I still love to eat in the trattorie.

AMA: Me too. It's much more genuine. Sometimes I'll read the menu of a Michelin star place and think that's not really what I would like to eat, to be quite honest.

I've eaten at some really beautiful places in Milano and have left not really remembering what I've eaten. We used to eat a lot at the bocciofila in an old working class neighbourhood: it was just a woman making all the meals and I still remember exactly what I ate every day.

AMA: Oh yes. Those are the best places.

Is there anything like that here?

AMA: Apart from Zucca? [laughs] There used to be a place on St. Clair and Dufferin where a Roman woman was cooking. I used to just stop there and try whatever that woman was cooking. It felt very honest and very unique. That kind of food is getting harder and harder to find. The Portuguese had done it. They had all of their lunch places. We're getting more and more hung up on these amazing young chefs who are cooking for a young, 20-something crowd. The music is loud and it's crowded. But that is a lifestyle.

Would you like to add any fond memory?

AMA: I remember Ada Boni. She was the Italian equivalent of Julia Child and *Mastering the Art of French Cooking*. She started writing in the 30s or 40s. Her first cookbook, *Talismano della felicità* was geared to housewives. It was genuine regional food and it had the most amazing photographs. It had a genuine history with beautiful landscapes. It was fantastic.

Was it in English?

AMA: I read it in English, but then I managed to get an Italian copy. She was my first source for Italian cooking.

Do you still refer to her?

AMA: If I want to look at making a Roman baccalà or something, I will look to her. She is sort of like the Bible to me.